STOP SMOKING NOW

2nd Edition

*A self-help guide using
cognitive behavioural techniques*

OVERCOMING

DAVID F MARKS

ROBINSON

ROBINSON

First published in Great Britain in 2017 by Robinson

Copyright © David F Marks, 2017

1 3 5 7 9 10 8 6 4 2

A CIP catalogue record for this book
is available from the British Library.

Important Note
This book is not intended as a substitute for medical advice or treatment.
Any person with a condition requiring medical attention should consult a
qualified medical practitioner or suitable therapist.

ISBN: 978-1-47213-865-1

Typeset in Bembo by Initial Typesetting Services, Edinburgh
Printed and bound in Great Britain by Clays Ltd, St Ives plc

MIX
Paper from
responsible sources
FSC® C104740
www.fsc.org

Robinson
An imprint of
Little, Brown Book Group
Carmelite House
50 Victoria Embankment
London EC4Y 0DZ

An Hachette UK Company
www.hachette.co.uk

www.littlebrown.co.uk

Contents

PART THREE
LIVING AS A NON-SMOKER

Introduction

In my twenties virtually everybody was smoking. Smoking was the natural and normal thing to do. You could smoke almost anywhere. In shops, cafes, pubs, clubs, cinemas, theatres, absolutely everywhere. It seems crazy now, but that's how it was. I was a pack-a-day smoker and guess what; I actually thought I was enjoying it. Sound familiar?

Cigarette advertising was everywhere. In newspapers, magazines, on TV, at the movies and on huge advertising boards all over the place. People would literally drive along motorways smoking cigarettes and crash their cars gawping at the ads. It seems a different reality now, but that's exactly how it was. All kinds of subtle and clever messages designed to get everybody to smoke a particular brand. Brands for ladies, brands for teens, brands for minorities, brands for everyone.

By 1976, I was living in the USA, and had probably been smoking for about ten or eleven years. I had tried several brands but usually drifted back to one favourite. I had tried to move to a supposedly safer 'low tar' version of that brand (before advertising of misleading labels for 'light', 'low' and 'mild' cigarettes was banned in America), but found that a week or two after I had made the switch, I woke with an unexplained headache and I began to notice that I had to inhale very deeply to get any real satisfaction. I was working at the University of Oregon with a very famous psychologist, Professor Ray Hyman. Ray Hyman remains one of the tiny number of people to have one of the few real 'laws' in the science of psychology named after him: the Hick-Hyman Law. Ray is an extremely smart and erudite guy who knows a lot about a lot and I greatly respect and admire him.

One evening over dinner Ray gave me a penetrating stare and said: 'Given all you know about the ill-effects of smoking, why the heck are you still smoking?' He stopped me dead, so to speak. I really couldn't give a rational answer. It was at that very moment that I decided to give up smoking. Within a few days of preparation, I did it. I destroyed my remaining cigarettes and never smoked again.

As I sit at my laptop, forty years later, I can honestly say that I gave up smoking thanks to the headaches from my low tar cigarettes and the pep talk from my friend. My thanks go out to them both. This was the best health-related decision that I took in the whole of my life. It's now forty short years since I quit smoking.

Once I took the decision to quit smoking, however, it was far from plain sailing. I discovered how very difficult it can be. I was crotchety with the whole world. I couldn't sleep properly. I was sharing my woes with the inside of a beer bottle. There was an inexplicable gap in my life. A vacuum of nothingness that was difficult to fill.

This was how it all started, the main reason I decided to write books and run programmes and campaigns to help other people to stop smoking. After I returned to New Zealand from my visit to the US, a very smart PhD student at Otago University who I was supervising, called Paul Sulzberger, came to me with the idea. He and I started running Stop Smoking courses. We put together a course of five sessions that groups of people attended over a period of eight days. The sessions started on a Tuesday and finished the following Wednesday. It was highly successful. Eighty-five percent of smokers had given up by the end of the eight days. The remaining 15 percent had all reduced their consumption.

News of our Stop Smoking programme spread like wildfire and we took the programme all over New Zealand and into Australia. We must have helped twenty-thousand-plus smokers give up the habit. Our research and an independent research organisation told us that we were producing some very exciting results, the highest cessation rates ever recorded. We did ads on TV and in the major papers and franchised the system internationally and it is still running under various umbrellas to this day.

In the mid-1980s I moved to London as head and the first Professor of Psychology at the School of Psychology at Middlesex Polytechnic. The busy London lifestyle felt a bit different to laid-back New Zealand. In my efforts to continue the march against smoking, I needed a more efficient approach so I converted the method into a self-help pack I called the Quit for Life Programme. This was published by the British Psychological Society. Then, in 2005, the first edition of this book was published. In its current edition, *Stop Smoking Now* has proved to be one of the most successful stop smoking systems ever invented. I have the results of scientific trials that prove this.

One of my most memorable moments was when I visited the beautiful South Island of New Zealand on holiday with my son, Mike. While in Dunedin we visited a friend at St Clair. It was a warm and sunny afternoon. A person I did not remember at first, who had taken our stop smoking programme many years before, came over and looked me straight in the eye. She said, 'You saved my life. You helped me stop smoking twenty-five years ago. Now I'm seventy-five and fit as a fiddle, thanks to you, I wouldn't still be here if you hadn't helped me stop smoking.'

This is not the only time I have heard the heart-warming announcement, 'You saved my life.' Many others have said exactly the same thing. That's not why I studied psychology, to save lives, but that's precisely what it's ended up being.

I probably wouldn't still be alive today myself if I hadn't stopped smoking in my thirties. I know this from bitter experience. I watched my only brother Jon die from throat cancer caused by smoking. I tried to persuade him to quit but he would not listen to my pleading. He had other problems too, especially drinking. It was part of his trade as a jazz musician. Jon only reached his sixtieth birthday. My uncle Geoff, another smoker, also died from cancer.

But that's all history now. Let's return to the present. This book is about you.

You are on a different path, a path that will lead to improved health, improved well-being, and happiness. Please carry on reading and learn how to *Stop Smoking Now.*

Preface

Welcome to *Stop Smoking Now!* One of the most important decisions you have ever taken or will ever take is to stop smoking now.

If you're a smoker and want to stop the habit, this book is for you.

Read this book, absorb what's inside, and you will never be the same person.

Not many books can truthfully say this but this book really could save your life. This book definitely offers you a healthier and longer life. It also could save you a shed-load of money. A new car every year, fabulous holidays, and a much higher quality of life are all yours if you really want them. But it isn't really about the money. It's about your health and well-being. Are you ready for all this?

To gain these benefits, all you need to do for the next seven to ten days is to follow the process. Yes, that's right, it really is that simple. Hard to believe, right?

Well, consider this. I have spent the last forty years fine-tuning the best possible ways for smokers to overcome the habit. This experience has led to the current format that is *Stop Smoking Now*. My role as a health psychologist has brought me into contact with people from many backgrounds and cultures who have been at all the different stages of stopping smoking. In many cases, the smokers started out as desperate and hopeless cases, feeling that nothing could work for them. They had tried everything, but nothing had succeeded. Instead of blaming the faulty systems they had been using to stop smoking, including most of all, their own willpower, they blamed themselves. They blamed themselves for being 'weak'. Sounds familiar?

All a person needs to stop smoking is a system that actually works. A week or two weeks of serious application and, bingo, you will hit the jackpot, stop smoking, and remain a non-smoker for the rest of your life. Like many ex-smokers, you will experience feelings of joy, empowerment and hugely increased well-being by achieving what previously seemed impossible – stopping smoking. Nothing can offer you a greater boost to your self-esteem than to stop smoking, absolutely nothing. It's better than winning the lottery. Because it's not just about the money you'll save, it's about a whole new you.

This book gives you the most effective method of stopping smoking. The processes described here will enable you to bring about the change.

I know – I have been there!

What you need to stop smoking now

You have taken the first precious step on the path to changing your smoking habit. You now have within your hands a powerful and unique system designed to enable you to reach this important goal to stop smoking. You have the desire. You have the motivation. You have the ability. This book gives you the strategies, the know-how that you need to stop smoking now. Follow the guidance in this book, and you will stop smoking in just a few days and, think about it, you will never need to smoke again!

This will be the most important step to improve your health that you can take in the whole of your life. Experiencing the process from beginning to end is something you will never forget. You will be a changed person, a *new you*.

You already realise that smoking is the most stupid, addictive and harmful habit known to humankind. It is predicted that one billion people will die in the twenty-first century as a consequence of smoking. *One way of solving the world's population explosion, I suppose* . . . But a smoking -related death is not normally a quick death. Smoking-related illnesses are nasty, protracted and painful and require thousands of pounds in health care. Having watched my brother die slowly, in great pain, it's something I wouldn't wish on anybody.

This book offers you the best chance to overcome your smoking habit. It offers you a way to extinguish the habit, once and for all. And that's without taking a shed-load of gut-busting drugs. The methods in this book have been evaluated with hundreds of smokers in randomised, controlled trials. Tens of thousands of people like you have successfully overcome their smoking habit using these methods.

If you use all of the procedures with commitment and perseverance, you will overcome your smoking habit for ever. You will be a calm and confident non-smoker.

Stop Smoking Now is in three stages. Part One is all about theory. I discuss the psychology of smoking and quitting. I introduce Cognitive Behavioural Therapy (CBT) and its cousin, mindfulness, explain how they work and how they can help you to give up smoking once and for all. I will help you to think about what you do when you smoke, why you do it, and what smoking really means to you.

However, if you're not much interested in theory and want to cut straight to the nitty-gritty, you can skip Part One and move directly to Part Two.

Part Two is the practical stuff, the guts of the whole system. It guides you, step by step, from the addicted smoker you are now to a new, healthy life as a non-smoker. The process takes seven to ten days. This will be your new beginning, the most dramatic way to improve your quality of life, extend your lifespan and make you better off financially in one smart move.

Part Three is also practical. It's about regaining your life as a non-smoker. It guides you over the pitfalls of being a recent quitter and helps you to prevent relapse and maintain your non-smoking permanently.

Let *Stop Smoking Now* be your guide and you will never need anything else. Other stop-smoking books make false and highly exaggerated claims and have never been properly tested.

Why you should stop smoking now

Stopping smoking is, without any doubt, the most important thing you can do to improve your health. If you stop
smoking:

- You will live a longer and healthier life.
- You will significantly reduce your chance of having a
  heart attack, stroke or cancer.
- Your skin, hair, body and clothes will no longer reek
  of tobacco.
- Your fingers will stop turning yellow.
- Your sex life will show a significant improvement.
- If you are pregnant, you will improve your chances
  of having a healthy baby.
- The people you live with, your loved ones and
  your children, will have a healthier, less polluted
  environment.
- You will save a lot of extra money to spend on luxur-
  ies and holidays.

How this method can help you

Part One introduces the main ideas behind smoking addiction, and the theory and research that support *Stop Smoking
Now* as the best available method for quitting smoking.

Part Two contains thirty different procedures that have
helped thousands of smokers give up the habit. Nobody
can predict which particular procedures will work best for

you – everybody is different. However, by trying this wide range of different procedures, you are giving yourself your best chance of success. Please try them all.

Believe it or not, you can possibly enjoy certain aspects of the process of stopping smoking. It is part of the design to make this method as enjoyable and fun an experience as possible. You will learn a lot about yourself and the potential you have to change yourself for the better. Yes, to actually make yourself a better and more aware and fully functioning person! But I would not be telling you the whole truth, if I didn't tell you that it can be very, very difficult. You already know that.

An addicted smoker is always, to a degree, dysfunctional. The changes that you make will help you to be a fully functional human being again. Like you used to be before you took up the habit, or rather, before the habit took over you.

Drinking, eating, internet-surfing, shopping, chilling, watching TV, gaming, gambling – anything to excess can quickly turn into an addiction. Smoking is a habit which seems extremely difficult to change. As an ex-smoker I know. But smoking can be brought under control easily and permanently by applying this systematic programme.

The book can be used as a stand-alone, self-help, how-to method of quitting or it can be combined with the treatment offered by your local health service providers. Two or more smokers can also work through *Stop Smoking Now* together to generate an element of cooperation, or even competition. 'Who gets there first?' is always an interesting challenge, as is 'Who stays there the longest?'

Social media

Stop Smoking Now is also available on a range of social media. Feel free to join the *Stop Smoking Now* community at these different sites to chat, comment or ask questions. I will drop by on a regular basis to answer your queries and offer personalised advice.

YouTube www.youtube.com/channel/UCUjvqQ4Zkaoz kIbGUh2X_lw

Facebook www.facebook.com/StopSmokingNowTheProcess/

Twitter twitter.com/SSNTHEPROCESS/

I look forward to meeting you!

Practical advice

The techniques of *Stop Smoking Now* were first published by the British Psychological Society in 1993 as *The Quit for Life Programme*. Viewed by the society as the most effective method for stopping smoking, it has been evaluated in several scientifically controlled trials. Full details of the results of the research, the clinical trials and reviews can be found in the Useful References section at the end of this book.

Stop Smoking Now offers proven techniques from the toolboxes of Cognitive Behaviour Therapy and mindfulness. It is different from other methods because it engages you as a whole person. It also differs from almost all other methods in recommending a gradual tapering off of cigarette consumption over a week to ten days. The most important difference is that *Stop Smoking Now* actually works. It is also, with a few exceptions, entirely drug-free. Scientific research suggests that the system can be used by everybody, regardless of their education, income or social background.

All you need is motivation and the ability to read.

In order to obtain the maximum benefit from this book, please follow the instructions step by step, until you reach your final Stop-Day.

Other methods claim high success rates but without properly controlled trials to support those claims. This sad fact is typical of the whole area of self-help books on smoking. No other self-help book currently on the market has scientific trials proving effectiveness.

Don't believe the hype. There are smoke and mirrors everywhere.

Many methods on the market are no more successful than just stopping smoking by yourself. The truth is, that is how the vast majority of smokers do stop: completely on their own, without any outside help.

The typical method tries to build up the smoker's motivation to the point where she or he is meant to stop smoking *instantaneously*, by the strength of will. Using willpower is unlikely to be the best way. Perhaps combined with special drugs, the smoker is meant to make a permanent transformation? The smoker is expected to think and feel a completely different person purely by making a decision to do so. Doesn't sound very plausible, does it? The whole idea is absurd, as is hypnosis. There are a lot desperate and gullible people who will grab at any straws to stop smoking. Never trust anybody who says they can stop you smoking with hypnosis. It simply doesn't work in the long term.

Stop Smoking Now offers you effective methods of change. It offers you methods to change feelings, thoughts and behaviours about smoking over a period of seven to ten days. You will return to an earlier state of being nicotine-free, something from an earlier stage of life, before you became a smoker.

We know that your habit built up over many years or even decades and cannot disappear overnight. You need time to change and time to recondition your thoughts and feelings. This is a rekindling of a previous identity, a newly refreshed vision of you. This cannot be done simply by taking a miraculous decision to do so. Anybody who believes in that kind of cartoon magic belongs in Disney World, not the real world.

Yet this is what the traditional methods expect of you: they tell you to stop at a certain date and then expect it will just miraculously happen. Now if that could be achieved permanently that really would indeed be a miracle. Haven't you already tried that? And haven't you discovered that miracles simply do not happen? No wonder the results from such traditional 'willpower' procedures are so notoriously poor. They are based on ludicrous assumptions that have no foundation in the science of psychology – or even in common sense.

Overcoming smoking takes time. Not necessarily a very long time, but over a week to ten days. It is you who decides when you will smoke and when you will stop smoking. It is you and you alone. As if it could ever be any other way. This book tells you exactly what you need to do in an easy, step-by-step programme.

First of all, it gives you the necessary mental preparation. You can't swim before you can paddle. You don't need to be thrown into the deep end because you might drown. Let's go at it in a steady and sure fashion.

Softly, softly, catchee monkey . . .

Two golden rules

You will continue to smoke during the first few days of the programme. To aid your success, here are two simple 'golden rules':

Golden Rule one: smoke every time you feel like smoking, right up to your final Stop-Day.

Golden Rule two: use the recommended procedures whenever you smoke or feel like smoking.

The exercises offered in Parts Two and Three give you all the ammunition you need to destroy your smoking habit once and for all. You need to read the contents and follow the advice step-by-step as systematically as possible.

There are relevant factors that you need to take into account before you begin.

Timing

Timing is of the essence. Probably you have chosen to

read this book because you have the time and have seen an opportunity to stop smoking now. At certain times, circumstances preclude making such a major change. For example, changing jobs, going through a separation or divorce, or suffering a bereavement or other trauma are definitely not suitable times to attempt to stop smoking. If any of these scenarios apply to you, then put this book aside and return to it when there are no longer such major distractions.

It takes a period of focused effort to quit smoking successfully. If you are going through other major changes at the same time, you won't be able to make the necessary effort to quit smoking as well. It would be better to wait until things settle down before embarking upon this programme.

One easy-to-arrange factor is the day of week when you begin the programme. Experience suggests that it is better to make some initial progress over the main part of the week first, then to tackle the weekend. For many people the weekend is different from the Monday-to-Friday routine so, when you are in the middle of quitting smoking, the weekend will need special planning. If you are on shift work or working part-time at home you need to decide on the best time within your schedule to carry out this seven to ten day programme.

Without any doubt, the best day to begin this programme is a Tuesday. You will be able to reduce your cigarette consumption to manageable proportions by the weekend. You will also avoid the 'Monday effect' – the extra stress and hassle Monday brings after a hopefully more leisurely Saturday and Sunday. It's also a good idea to steer clear of weeks ending in long weekends or special occasions such as Christmas, new year and other festivals and holidays, because you need to quit when things are relatively normal and routine. That gives you the best chance to quit smoking.

Motivation

Motivation is a major factor. A smoker's desire to quit waxes and wanes, but the best time for you to quit is when you really want to stop. Simply being persuaded, nagged, or cajoled to do so by another person is definitely not enough. Of course, everybody who cares about you should want you to quit and should encourage and support you while you are doing so. But you have to really want to stop smoking for yourself, not for anybody else: only you can make the conscious decision that now is the time to quit and you're going to do it.

In thinking about your motives, consider three things: your health, your attractiveness, and your wealth. Firstly, your health. The health effects of smoking are well known; they are discussed further in chapter one. Secondly, attractiveness. Smoking may have seemed a cool thing to do when you first started, but nowadays it's uncool. Apart from anything else, your body, breath, hair and clothes stink. If you carry on smoking, you will wrinkle at a younger age and age more quickly.

Thirdly, consider your pocket. Currently, a packet of twenty cigarettes costs around £9.60 in the UK. If you have a twenty-a-day habit, you're burning £3,500 per year (January 2016 prices). Over twenty-five years, that's £87,600, plus the interest, which at only 2 per cent comes to £26,848, giving you a total saving of £117,848. Now, if the price of cigarettes doubles over that period, which is highly likely, so does the amount you would save. You could save around a quarter of a million pounds, the price of a house! Wow, think of that – a house gone up in smoke – what a bum deal!

In the US, the price of cigarettes varies state by state. For example, in New York a packet of Marlboro Reds costs $14.50 but in Kentucky it costs only $4.96 (12 July 2013). A New Yorker would burn $5,300 in one year, producing a saving of $178,456 over twenty-five years, which doubles to $357,000.

Think what you could do with that kind of money . . . write down now a bucket list of what you would do with a quarter or a third of a million . . . You probably don't need much more persuading than this.

Working through the process

Part One introduces smoking addiction and the psychological theory that lies behind my method for stopping smoking. To gain maximum results, please read the whole book all the way through in a systematic manner. You need to clear your schedule to read at least one chapter a day for the next ten days. If you follow all the procedures as directed on a day-by-day basis, you will be able to stop smoking easily and permanently.

There are thirty or more different procedures that have all been tried and tested by thousands of smokers. Nobody can predict which aspects will work best for you or which methods you will find the most useful – everybody is different. However, by trying this wide range, you will give yourself the best chance of success. The results from thousands of other successful ex-smokers prove this.

Although you need to make an effort and focus on stopping smoking for seven to ten days, believe it or not, you can actually enjoy the process! Not all of it, all of the time, for sure, but at least parts of it. Smoking is a habit which seems extremely difficult to change but it can be brought under control permanently by applying this systematic psychological programme of CBT and mindfulness.

You can actually have fun dealing with the challenges you will face and mastering the techniques, and you will learn a lot about yourself in the process. You will discover your potential to change your own behaviours. Drinking, eating, shopping, lounging, watching the television, gambling – anything done to excess can become an addiction. If any of these things are also a problem, put them to one side until after you have conquered smoking. Then when you've got smoking firmly under your control, you may decide to tackle one of these other things, if it is actually becoming a concern.

Summary

- Start the process of quitting when your life is running on a fairly even course.
- You will need to allocate one hour a day for one week to ten days to complete the process.
- Do this for you, because *you* really want to, not because you want to please somebody who's been nagging you to stop. It happens.
- Prepare yourself by reading each chapter of the book the day before you need to use it. So on Tuesday evening, read the chapter for Wednesday, on Wednesday read the chapter for Thursday, and so on.
- Start only when you are prepared to really work at it.
- Golden Rule one tells you to smoke every time you feel like smoking, right up to your final Stop-Day. You will continue to smoke during the first part of the programme.
- Golden Rule two tells you carry out the procedures whenever you smoke or feel like smoking.
- Do your homework and the procedures will do wonders for you.
- Enjoy the process. Making the changes that you most desire can be very exciting. Nothing more so than stopping smoking.

I wish you complete success in becoming a happy and successful non-smoker.

Acknowledgements

Many people and organisations have provided their support during the development of *Stop Smoking Now.* The book is based on research and development over a period of 40 years. I warmly thank Paul Sulzberger who co-developed the precursor of *Stop Smoking Now* when we both were at the University of Otago, New Zealand in 1977. Paul, it was your amazing energy and enthusiasm that helped pave the way to a new 'Non-smoking utopia' that New Zealand is fast becoming. New Zealand now has one of the lowest smoking rates anywhere in the developed world.

I warmly thank Kathleen Campbell, David Carter, Lati Haddad, Ian Hodgson, Gillian Pow and Margaret McGoldrick for their invaluable support as we nurtured this project through its infancy. To Susan Pacitti, previously at BPS Books, for editing and locating an obscure track of baroque music needed for the audio recording. Stuart Macgregor, after a chance meeting in Edinburgh, kindly provided cartoons for which I am eternally grateful.

Catherine Sykes for organisational skills, expertise and enthusiasm in taking the process through adolescence and one step closer to its current format.

The now defunct Health Education Authority gave permission to reprint extracts from *Enjoy Healthy Eating* (in chapter 10) and *Exercise Why Bother?* (in chapter 11). I have retained these extracts with a tip of the hat to the staff at the HEA.

I am pleased to acknowledge Mark Williams, John Teasdale, Zindel Segal, and Jon Kabat-Zinn for the Raisin Exercise reproduced in Chapter 10 from their book, *The Mindful Way through Depression: Freeing Yourself from Chronic Unhappiness* (Guilford Press, 2007). Meditation has been a part of the programme that is *Stop Smoking Now* since 1977. However, the addition of theoretical ideas concerning mindfulness as a way of improving awareness of being is new to this edition.

I also happily acknowledge the inspiration of *The Chimp Paradox* (Vermilion, 2012) by Professor Steve Peters of the University of Sheffield. The model of the brain in *Stop Smoking Now* is adapted from the triune brain theory of Paul D. MacLean. 'The biocomputer' in *Stop Smoking Now* predates Professor Peters' 'Computer' by thirty-five years. However, 'The chimp' in *Stop Smoking Now* is new and, in many ways, resembles the 'Chimp' described by Steve Peters. We both talk about 'Autopilots', mine appearing as 'The chameleon'. Parallels in content stop there. There is no Chameleon in *The Chimp Paradox* and no 'Gremlins', 'Goblins' or 'Stone of life' in *Stop Smoking Now*. Also I don't exercise, box or give bananas to my Chimp. I was always taught that reward works better than punishment but I suspect that bananas, exercise and being boxed only work short-term. Reportedly, Professor Peters was Roy Hodgson's 'secret weapon' at the Euro 2016 Championship,

ACKNOWLEDGEMENTS

so I'd better not mention the Iceland vs England game, England's quick exit, and the indifferent performances by the players. Nobody is perfect. My Chimp changes its behaviour by reprogramming, with more lasting impact, I believe.

In regard to sources, it isn't appropriate to cite chapter and verse. *Stop Smoking Now* is a how-to book for smokers who don't want references, just practical help. However, a set of Useful References and Websites appears at the back.

In publishing with Little, Brown, I am happy to sit in the company of some the world's most inspiring writers, such as Louisa M. Alcott, C. S. Forester, John Fowles, Malcolm Gladwell, Norman Mailer, Nelson Mandela, Masters and Johnson, Gore Vidal, J. K. Rowling, P. G. Wodehouse and James Patterson. Although the how-to genre may not be quite to everybody's literary tastes, I'd rather have a crack at a how-to book that improves lives than be idle. Thank you Little, Brown and the Robinson imprint, you have been wonderful. To everybody who has contributed, I offer my sincere thanks.

Lastly, warm thanks to Alice Vallat for offering the perfect writer's home in Provence.

David F Marks

Disclaimer

The system described in this book was previously called *The Quit for Life Programme* when published by the British Psychological Society (Marks, 1993). The name 'Quit for Life' was also taken by an unrelated organisation in the USA (American Cancer Society's Quit For Life Program). In addition, Southern Health NHS Foundation Trust, based in Hampshire, England, took the name 'Quit4Life' for its Stop Smoking Service. The system that is now called Stop Smoking Now, as described in this book, is independent of these other organisations and the content of this book is different and unique and is subject to the laws of copyright throughout the world.

This book is designed to provide information and education to our readers. It is sold with the understanding that the publisher is not engaged to render any type of psychological, legal, or any other kind of professional advice. The content is the sole expression and opinion of its author, and not necessarily that of the publisher. Neither the publisher nor the individual author shall be liable for any physical, psychological, emotional, financial, or commercial damages, including, but not limited to, special, incidental, consequential or other damages. Our views and rights are the same: you are responsible for your own choices, actions, and results.

PART ONE

UNDERSTANDING SMOKING AND STRATEGIES FOR STOPPING

Part One presents the theory and evidence behind the process of stopping smoking as described in detail in Part Two. If you don't need or want to know about theory and evidence, then please jump straight to Part Two.

Chapter 1 describes how and why smoking becomes an addiction. Chapter 2 discusses the disadvantages of nicotine replacement therapy, E-cigarettes and anti-smoking medication. Chapter 3 describes effective practical methods for stopping smoking, cognitive behavioural therapy and mindfulness. When you have mastered these, you will have mastered your addiction to nicotine.

1

Understanding smoking addiction

How many people smoke?

Approximately one in five of the world's adult population smokes cigarettes. That's over 1.1 billion people. In the UK there are about ten million smokers and in the US there are around forty million. Smoking is on the decline in many countries but smoking rates appear to be increasing in the eastern Mediterranean area and Africa. Tobacco is the last thing anybody needs, never mind impoverished people, but aggressive marketing by Big Tobacco is pushing smoking, whether they want it or not.

The World Health Organisation (WHO) estimates that 47 per cent of men and 12 per cent of women smoke. Although fewer women currently are smokers than men, there have been dramatic increases in smoking among women and, in most places, the consumption gap between men and women is narrowing. More aggressive marketing by Big Tobacco.

Compared to the rest of the world, Europe still has one of the highest proportions of deaths attributable to tobacco.

Sixteen per cent of all adult deaths in the WHO European region were due to tobacco. In Europe, 22 per cent of women smoke: a high average compared to those for women in Africa, Asia and the Middle East (3–5 per cent). Higher death rates in these latter regions will kick in after a generation of chronic tobacco use. If it is left unchecked, it has been predicted that tobacco will kill one billion people in the twenty-first century. I hope that you will not be one of them!

What's in cigarette smoke?

More than seven thousand chemicals, including forty-three known cancer-causing compounds, are found in tobacco smoke. Cigarettes contain small quantities of chemicals that are present in paint stripper, toilet cleaner, lighter fuel, mothballs, gas chambers, and rocket fuel. These include nicotine, tar, and carbon monoxide, formaldehyde, ammonia, hydrogen cyanide, arsenic, and DDT.

The only reason anybody smokes cigarettes is to obtain nicotine. That's because nicotine is highly addictive. It's one of nature's most addictive substances. The other chemicals in cigarettes have been added for 'technical reasons', to help the cigarette burn in the right way, to make the tobacco taste good and to add to its shelf-life. Two well-known poisons are arsenic and strychnine. Believe it or not, nicotine is more poisonous than both of them. The amount of the substance in hand-rolling tobacco is higher than in manufactured cigarettes, but the tar in tobacco smoke is the single most important health risk.

What's in cigarette smoke?
(Reproduced by permission from the American Lung Association)

What are the health effects of smoking?

You know already the terrible health effects of smoking. I make no apology for highlighting a few key points to remind you why you're here.

The health effects of smoking have been studied for over one hundred years. Even Big Tobacco now admits the health dangers of smoking. The Centers for Disease Control and Prevention (CDC) in the US offer a guide to the health impacts of smoking. If you're interested in the science of tobacco and smoking, there is plenty of information at the CDC website at: www.cdc.gov/tobacco

Smoking accounts for 440,000 deaths each year in the US and 120,000 deaths in the UK, nearly one in five of all deaths. More deaths are caused each year by tobacco than all deaths from HIV, illegal drug use, alcohol, motor vehicle injuries, suicides, and murders combined. Men who smoke cut their lives short on average by thirteen years and female smokers lose fourteen and a half years. The risk of dying from lung cancer is twenty-two times higher among men who smoke, and twelve times higher among women who smoke, compared with those who have never smoked. Alarming!

About 80 per cent of adult smokers start smoking before the age of eighteen. You probably did yourself. Every day thousands of teenagers – and even some pre-teens – try their first cigarette. Like lambs to the slaughter. These unsuspecting victims have been successfully recruited by Big Tobacco to replace the unfortunates who've already passed away. The system operates a bit like a corner sweet-shop before school – one out, one in. Early addiction to smoking often leads to illness in later life and an early death. Millions of children living today will die prematurely because of their decision to smoke cigarettes. All under the watchful eye of Big Tobacco, forever chasing bigger profits for its shareholders. Even now as Big Tobacco has found a new way to make people addicted to nicotine – the e-cigarette.

A report in 1964 from the US surgeon general showed that smoking was a definite cause of cancers of the lung and larynx (voice box) in men and chronic bronchitis in both men and women. Later reports concluded that smoking causes diseases such as cancers of the bladder, oesophagus, mouth and throat; cardiovascular diseases; and reproductive effects. The list was expanded to include illnesses and conditions linked to smoking such as cataracts, pneumonia, acute myeloid leukaemia, abdominal aortic aneurysm, stomach cancer, pancreatic cancer, cervical cancer, kidney cancer and periodontitis.

The earlier in life that you can stop smoking, the better off you will be when you are older. One of the main excuses people give for not stopping is that it is too late for them. Please don't be fooled into thinking this. It is never too late to stop smoking. Unless of course, you are already almost dead with the effects of a horrible condition such as emphysema. Then it really is too late and even your own doctor will condone your smoking.

Smoking causes immediate damage to your body that can lead to long-term health problems. For every smoking-related death, at least thirty people live with a smoking-related illness. Cigarette smokers are two to four times more likely to develop coronary heart disease than non-smokers. Smoking approximately doubles a person's risk for stroke and causes reduced circulation by narrowing the blood vessels (arteries). Smokers are more than ten times as likely as non-smokers to develop peripheral vascular disease.

Smoking is associated with a ten-fold increase in the risk of dying from chronic obstructive lung disease (COPD). About 90 per cent of all deaths from COPD are attributable to cigarette smoking. Cigarette smoking has many adverse reproductive and early childhood effects, including an increased risk for infertility, pre-term delivery, stillbirth, low

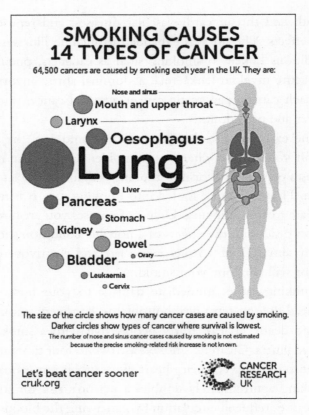

The fourteen main types of cancer caused by smoking.
(Reproduced by permission from Cancer Research UK)

birth-weight, and sudden infant death syndrome (SIDS). Postmenopausal women who smoke have lower bone density than women who have never smoked. Women who smoke have an increased risk for hip fracture than those who have never smoked.

As one would expect, tobacco smoke does most damage to the person who is actively inhaling. However, those nearby are breathing second-hand or environmental tobacco smoke (ETS) and they too also have a higher risk of cancer, heart disease, and respiratory disease, as well as sensory irritation. Scientific evidence suggests that smoking causes the premature death of hundreds of thousands of non-smokers worldwide. A woman's risk of developing lung cancer is raised by 26 per cent when exposed to the side-stream smoke of a husband who is a smoker. It's best to think twice before marrying a smoker! There is a relationship between the risk of lung cancer and the number of cigarettes smoked by a person's partner in addition to the length of time the person has been exposed to their smoke. Long-term exposure of non-smokers to ETS causes an increased risk of lung cancer of 20 to 30 per cent. Until death us do part, with a vengeance!

The estimated increased risk equates to several hundred extra deaths per year in Britain. Smoking by parents also causes acute and chronic middle ear disease in children. SIDS, the main cause of post-neonatal death in the first year of life, is also associated with exposure to environmental tobacco smoke.

Cigarettes are the major cause of fires in domestic, industrial and public buildings. Tobacco smoke cannot be controlled by ventilation, air cleaning or by separating smokers from non-smokers. Making public places smoke-free is the only real remedy, something that has happened in many countries over the last decade. This has resulted in increasing feelings of stigma for smokers and a build-up of social pressure from family, friends and workmates to stop. Probably that's one reason you're here right now.

What is Nicotine?

It is well-established that the addictiveness of tobacco is centred on the nicotine. The tobacco plant has many species, some of which make a decorative flowering plant. The plant is a member of the genus *Nicotiana* of the *Solanaceae* (nightshade) family that also contains the potato. Tobacco is prepared by curing the leaves that are sticky to the touch with nicotine-containing resin.

Tobacco was an essential resource to British soldiers and sailors in the First World War. They smoked a thousand tons of cigarettes and seven hundred tons of pipe tobacco in 1915. Tobacco trade journals quoted from the medical journal *Lancet*: '*We may surely brush aside much prejudice against the use of tobacco when we consider what a source of comfort it is to the soldier and sailor engaged in a nerve-wracking campaign . . . tobacco fills an important place in the psycho-physiological affairs of the human race.*' It was widely thought that, for the troops fighting in the trenches, cigarettes were gifts of appreciation and, from family, of love.

Nicotine is a colourless liquid that turns brown when burned and smells of tobacco when exposed to air. It consists of 0.6–3.0 per cent of the dry weight of tobacco. Nicotine acts as a stimulant in small doses, but in larger amounts blocks the action of autonomic nerve and skeletal muscle

Nicotiana Sylvestris (flowering tobacco).

cells. Nicotine was once commonly used in insecticides. It is very toxic. The International Programme on Chemical Safety (IPCS) states, 'Nicotine is one of the most toxic of all poisons and has a rapid onset of action.'

It is so dangerous to gardeners that nicotine was removed as an insecticide in 2009, replaced by a new class of insecticide that share the same mode of action, the so-called 'neonicotinoids'. These are responsible for wiping out the bee population.

If you smoke a packet of twenty cigarettes in one go, it might actually kill you. It would certainly put you into hospital. Only by smoking cigarettes one at a time are you able to smoke them without risking dying on the spot. A fatal dose is around 0.5–1.0 gram of ingested nicotine.

Most cigarettes contain 10 milligrams or more of nicotine. The typical smoker takes in one to two milligrams of nicotine per cigarette. Nicotine is absorbed through the skin and lining of the mouth and nose or by inhalation in the lungs. For cigarettes, nicotine reaches peak levels in the bloodstream and brain within seven to ten seconds of inhalation. Cigar and pipe smokers, on the other hand, typically do not inhale the smoke, so nicotine is absorbed more slowly through the mucosal membranes of their mouths. Nicotine from smokeless tobacco is also absorbed through the mucosal membranes.

Nicotine has complex and sometimes unpredictable effects on the brain and body including:

- Decreases the appetite (good for trench warfare)
- Boosts in mood and sense of well-being (also good for trench warfare)
- Increases activity in the intestines (not so good for trench warfare)
- Creates more saliva and phlegm (ditto)
- Increases the heart rate by around ten to twenty beats per minute
- Increases blood pressure by 5 to 10 mmHg
- May cause sweating, nausea, and diarrhoea if taken to excess
- Stimulates memory and alertness

Nicotine in pregnancy

There is no doubt about it, smoking during pregnancy harms the baby in the womb from day one. In England, 11 per cent of mothers were recorded as smoking at time of delivery in 2015, a figure that varied between 2 per cent and 26 per cent across the country. It's not a good idea to smoke at all during pregnancy. Normal foetal development can be disrupted more by nicotine than by any other component of cigarette smoke. Nicotine could potentially even kill a foetus. Nicotine can affect the brain during critical stages of foetal development and most likely causes deficits in learning and memory and also emotional and behavioural problems in childhood and later in life.

There is now wide appreciation of the dangers of maternal smoking during pregnancy and the lifelong consequences this has on offspring lung function, including the increased risk of childhood wheezing and subsequent asthma. Recent evidence strongly supports that much of the effect of smoking during pregnancy on offspring lung function is mediated by nicotine, making it highly likely that e-cigarette use during pregnancy will have the same harmful effects on the lung function and health of offspring as do conventional cigarettes. In fact, the evidence for nicotine being the mediator of harm of conventional cigarettes may be most compelling for its effects on lung development.

A higher incidence of attention deficit hyperactivity disorder (ADHD), lower adult intelligence and mental retardation have been reported in nicotine-exposed offspring. When nicotine is present in the developing cortex during a critical period, it can permanently alter sensory-cognitive function. Nicotine exposure in pregnancy is responsible for auditory-cognitive deficits in the offspring. Children with cognitive hearing deficits have difficulty understanding speech in noisy settings and may be unable to tell the difference between similar sounds. Prenatal nicotine primes the adolescent brain for depression and for nicotine addiction in future years.

Aside from prenatal and postnatal nicotine exposure potentially causing sudden infant death syndrome (SIDS), yet another consequence is the incidence of low birth weight (LBW) babies, but even in the absence of LBW, nicotine affects foetal brain development and new-born behaviour. Nicotine concentrates in foetal blood, amniotic fluid and breast milk. Breast-feeding by smoking or ETS-exposed mothers continues the delivery of nicotine to the baby. Postnatal exposure to cigarette smoke also appears to act through nicotine: in a study of 4,399 children aged six to seventeen, even the lowest exposure was found to significantly impair the children's reading and reasoning scores.

During the first trimester, pregnant women need to avoid nicotine entirely. Avoiding nicotine throughout pregnancy would be the best option.

Nicotine in adolescence

The brain of a smoking teenager creates nerve cells to handle the flood of nicotine. As the number of receptor cells increases, a teenage smoker needs more nicotine to get the same kick. That makes the user seek hit after hit. Consequences such as impaired attention and bouts of depression or anxiety may follow. This makes adolescents more susceptible to nicotine dependence than adults. A single drug exposure can lead to lasting neuronal changes associated with learning and memory. The earlier the exposure to nicotine, the greater the impact on neuronal circuitry, causing irreversible effects on learning and memory. This experimental finding was borne out in a study where a single experience with cigarettes at age eleven was found to significantly increase the risk of becoming a smoker as an adolescent. Early exposure to nicotine can make children more vulnerable to stress or depression later in their lives, prompting them to try some form of nicotine again. We will need to raise the Red Danger Flag again in Chapter 2 when discussing the use of nicotine replacement therapy (NRT) and e-cigarettes in some detail.

What is addiction?

At any moment, around 70 per cent of smokers would say that they would like to quit. In any given year, approximately 50 per cent of all smokers will attempt to do so. Unfortunately, very few can actually succeed, less than 5 per cent. Why? It's simple – they are addicted. They are imprisoned in a jail called 'Nicotine Addiction' and they just don't know how to escape. You will receive your 'Get out of jail free' card very soon.

The only positive thing one can say about this situation is that the more times a smoker tries to quit, the greater their chances of success. It's a snowball effect. Lots of failures can lead to a success in the end, a bit like a lottery – the more tickets you buy, the greater your chances. A scientific approach is needed to minimise the chance element and to give you a decent stab at it.

Addiction occurs when an individual loses control over their behaviour, when an activity becomes compulsive. After you lose control, you are unable to contain the activity within reasonable bounds. The behaviour causes bad impacts on your life, health and well-being. You try to stop but, when you do so, there are unpleasant physical or mental consequences known as the 'withdrawal symptoms', including the craving, lack of concentration, unexplained grumpiness and so on.

Symptoms of nicotine withdrawal normally appear within two to three hours following your last smoke. People who smoked the most cigarettes or for the longest time generally suffer the worst withdrawal symptoms.

When you're in withdrawal, you'll probably notice one or more of the following:

- Craving for nicotine
- Feeling nervous (anxiety)
- Feeling low (depression)
- Feeling tense, restless, or frustrated (stress)
- Drowsiness and/or trouble sleeping
- Bad dreams and nightmares

- Headaches
- Increased appetite
- Problems concentrating

Smoking is on a par with heroin for addictiveness. I have encountered some extreme cases. A young man who worked as a waiter in a wine bar told me that he got through six packs (120 cigarettes!) every day! Yes, six whole packs! At first I could not understand this. Each cigarette takes, say, five minutes to smoke. If he smoked them one after the other, that would have meant six hundred minutes or ten hours of smoking each and every day. Here's how he did it. He explained that he would have several cigarettes alight at any one time, left in ashtrays at different tables, so he could be anywhere in the table area and be close enough to one somewhere in the room and be able to have a quick puff!

Another smoker told me that she set her alarm clock for 3.30 am every morning so she could have a cigarette to guarantee a decent night's sleep.

Another smoker told me that he smoked almost everywhere he went, including the shower. He kept a cigarette alight in a high-up soap dish so he could take a puff whenever he felt like it.

UK TV presenter Dale Winton told the London newspaper *Metro* that he was a thirty-a-day man. During an attack of bronchitis, he didn't smoke for eight days. This was an excellent opportunity to stop smoking altogether. However, Dale said that all he could think about was the fact that he wanted to get better – just so he could have a cigarette! Now that's addiction for you.

The fact that a smoker is able to smoke in so many different circumstances and situations is one of the main reasons smoking is such a difficult habit to break. Now here's an insight that you may never have thought of:

Every different situation in which you smoke is a separate smoking habit – smoking in the car, smoking in the street, smoking in the smoking room at work; smoking in each of these locations is a separate habit. The habit is created by a process of conditioning.

If smoking could be restricted to only one or two situations, the habit would be much easier to control. Conditioning sustains tobacco use through the reinforcing associations between smoking and triggers in the form of specific behaviours such as drinking coffee or alcohol, talking on the phone, driving a car and/or completing a meal. Such triggers are associated with the act of smoking and act as cues for smoking and maintain tobacco use. Research with cocaine and other drugs suggests that dopamine release occurs in the presence of these triggers alone. Simply experiencing a particular situation is sufficient to trigger a desire to smoke. This fact means that you are enslaved to smoke in many different situations. As a smoker, you are no longer free.

When you realise that your smoking is divided up into many different smoking habits, you have made a breakthrough. Each habit rests with a different trigger. They need to be eliminated, one by one. In Part Two we learn how.

How does addiction work?

Nicotine reaches the brain within seven seconds of inhaling. It heads straight towards brain cells that release dopamine. The smoker gains an immediate, feel-good high. After repeated exposures to nicotine, changes occur in the brain which interfere with the body's ability to release natural pleasure-giving chemicals on its own. The smoker then becomes dependent on the feel-good effects of nicotine to feel normal. Nicotine prison is only a few more cigarettes down the line. The unsuspecting rookie smoker will soon be locked way, possibly even for life.

The cigarette is a highly efficient system of drug-delivery. By inhaling, the smoker can get nicotine to the brain very rapidly with each and every puff. A typical smoker will take ten puffs on a cigarette during the five-minute period in which the cigarette is lit. Thus, a thirty-a-day smoker gets three hundred 'hits' of nicotine daily. That's over a hundred thousand hits a year, or one million hits every ten years. Quite a habit. This is one reason why smoking is so highly addictive. Smoking is rewarded hundreds of thousands of times over the smoker's lifetime. The reason you have become addicted to nicotine is that changes have occurred in your brain, so you require more nicotine to prevent withdrawal symptoms and to maintain an overall pleasant feeling. The process leads to a cycle of nicotine addiction, the prison that is smoking.

In the formation of tobacco addiction, the novice inhales tobacco smoke that, in the early stages, produces unpleasant sensations in the mouth and throat. However, with each inhalation, these unpleasant sensations are screened out and replaced by feelings of satisfaction as the addiction is formed. Feelings of satisfaction grow stronger as the habit is reinforced by the dopamine release and the experience of pleasure. As the habit strength increases, the smoker feels withdrawal symptoms that increase in intensity the longer he/she waits before lighting the next cigarette. Symptoms of addiction appear within a few days of occasional smoking. Before you know it, the jail door slams shut and you are back inside, in nicotine prison.

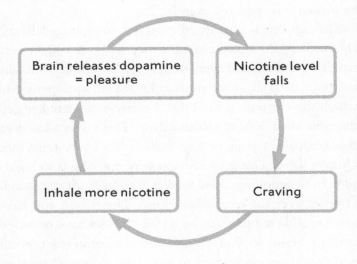

The cycle of nicotine addiction.

As an addicted prisoner of smoking, you know that nicotine can produce both pleasure and arousal. It pushes up your heart rate and your blood pressure. A cigarette kick lasts for only a few minutes before the craving starts to build up again. The smoker requires frequent top-ups of nicotine to maintain a state of stability. Over time, the smoker develops a tolerance to the arousing effects so that he or she requires more nicotine to maintain a feeling of 'normality' with the same neurochemical effect.

Nicotine addiction is a double-edged sword. It produces positive effects of pleasure and arousal and then, shortly afterwards, the unpleasant effects of nicotine withdrawal. Stopping smoking or waiting for longer between smokes causes withdrawal symptoms of irritability, anxiety, poor concentration, hunger, weight gain and problems getting along with others. The smoker needs cigarettes to regulate mood on a puff-by-puff basis. For this reason, smokers report that cigarettes help to relieve their feelings of stress. However, physiologically, a smoker's stress levels are higher than those of non-smokers and adolescent smokers report increasing levels of stress as they develop regular smoking patterns. The relaxation effect of smoking is a consequence of reversing the tension and irritability that develops between cigarettes. Exactly like any other addiction, smokers need nicotine to feel normal. The habit converts a free-thinking, free-acting human into a nicotine prisoner.

One mechanism common to all types of addiction is increased dopamine transmission, which gives an immediate feeling of pleasure and satisfaction. The increase in dopamine activity from nicotine results in pleasant feelings of satisfaction for the smoker, but the subsequent decrease in dopamine leaves the smoker craving for more cigarettes. Smoking, like all addictions, is a vicious circle.

Unfortunately, some smokers report increased coughing, throat soreness, chest problems and mouth ulcers after stopping. This deters them from continuing with their attempt to stop, providing an excuse to carry on smoking. Please be on your guard against this danger. Chapter 9 gives more details on how you can protect yourself against relapse.

You have a better chance of being successful if you have support

You can get support in many ways:

- Tell your family, friends, and colleagues that you are going to stop smoking and that you want their understanding and support. If any of them are smokers, ask them not to smoke around you or to leave cigarettes out.
- Talk to your doctor, dentist, nurse, pharmacist, psychologist or smoking counsellor. Inform them that you are using this book and ask them for their support.

There is an unpleasant craving that almost all smokers experience during the first few days or weeks after stopping. You can prevent craving, lapse and relapse by using a variety of methods. These methods are described in detail in Chapter 9. They have the advantage that they do not use drugs, so do not risk a new dependency on a different drug, have no side effects and can be considered to be less risky.

One common reason for restarting the habit is fear of weight gain. Many smokers gain weight when they stop. Eating a healthy diet and staying active are the two ways of dealing with this issue. Don't let weight gain distract you from your goal of stopping smoking. These issues will be discussed in detail in Chapters 10 and 11.

Can I use *Stop Smoking* Now while receiving other treatments?

Bear in mind that *Stop Smoking Now* offers different methods than other programmes. The main difference is that we recommend gradually reducing your smoking over several days. We call this 'tapering off'. Tapering is the best way because it gives you time to change the programmes in your mind that cause you to smoke in different trigger situations. To stop smoking, you must eliminate the causes. Anti-smoking clinics generally do not help you to discover and eliminate the causes. They use a shotgun pharmacy approach, a one-size-fits-all method that is rude and crude and very hit-and-miss.

Local health services generally provide the minimum level of support to would-be stoppers. The training of counsellors who run the smoking cessation services is psychologically superficial and does not include CBT. The training is aimed at minimising the problem of withdrawal by the use of medication. It usually does not attempt to give psychological support in the form of techniques. It is not surprising that many smokers treated by the health care system are dissatisfied with the service that they receive. The drop-out rate is very high, as is the relapse rate, at around 90 per cent. CBT methods improve the results of any treatment programme and complement the shotgun pharmacy approach that the clinics offer.

If you enrol for treatment in a clinic, then I strongly recommend that you apply *Stop Smoking Now* methodology before you reach your Stop-Day. This will enable you to minimise the drawbacks of using willpower and drugs. Using one drug to stop another drug is never a sensible policy. We discuss the futility of this in the next chapter. *Stop Smoking Now* teaches you how to control your smoking behaviour in a rational way. It will help to remove the pleasure and satisfaction that is being provided by smoking. It shows where your triggers are and how to eliminate them one by one. It frees your restless mind from the slavery of smoking.

For cannabis users only: can I stop smoking now but continue to smoke cannabis?

Many tobacco smokers also smoke cannabis. Cannabis is the most widely used recreational drug after tobacco and alcohol. In many states and countries it is now legal to use cannabis. In the UK, cannabis resin, or 'hash', is often mixed with tobacco in roll-ups, or joints. The smoker continues to smoke tobacco because he or she wishes to continue

24

smoking cannabis and thinks it's not possible to do one without doing the other.

This link between cannabis use and tobacco is unfortunate. Smoking is the most damaging way of using cannabis, because cannabis gives off three times as much tar and five times more carbon monoxide than average manufactured cigarettes. Whilst cannabis itself is not physically addictive, the nicotine in the tobacco is very addictive. For someone trying to stop smoking, mixing tobacco and cannabis is a very bad idea. It is possible to smoke or ingest cannabis without mixing it with tobacco. It is necessary that you do so.

A New Zealand study of the effects of tobacco and cannabis exposure on lung function in young adults looked at the use of cannabis and tobacco smoking at various ages. The subjects' lung function – the volume of air they could breathe out in one second – was tested. There was evidence of a linear relationship between cannabis use and lung function and daily cigarette smoking affected it even more. So using cannabis in smoked form may not be as safe as is often assumed by users.

Some studies suggest that smoking pure cannabis is more harmful to the lungs than tobacco. A study by the British Lung Foundation found that just three cannabis joints a day cause the same damage as twenty cigarettes. When cannabis and tobacco are smoked together, the effects are dramatically worse. Evidence shows that tar from cannabis cigarettes contains 50 per cent more cancer-causing carcinogens than tobacco.

Tetrahydocannibinol (THC) activates specific sites (called cannabinoid receptors) in the parts of the brain that influence pleasure, memory, thought, concentration, sensory and time perception and co-ordinated movement. Puff volume with cannabis is often three or four times higher than with tobacco – in other words, you inhale deeper and hold your breath with the smoke for longer before exhaling. This results in more carbon monoxide and tar entering into the lungs.

Many cannabis smokers become addicted to tobacco purely as a side effect of smoking cannabis. They would not consider themselves principally as tobacco smokers.

Practices vary across the world. Over 80 per cent of cannabis users in Britain smoke tobacco, either mixed with cannabis or by itself in cigarettes, when they finally realise they are tobacco addicts. Unfortunately, tobacco can make you an addict within a few tries and new smokers can then feel that they 'need' a joint, not realising that it is tobacco addiction kicking in. A new cannabis user will soon start smoking tobacco at regular intervals to maintain nicotine levels.

I have tried several times to help regular cannabis users break their nicotine addiction. It failed because they refused to stop smoking cannabis and tobacco together. If you are a regular cannabis user, then you must either stop using it or change the way you use cannabis if you are serious about giving up tobacco.

Conclusions

1. One in five of the adult population smokes. Three-quarters would like to stop but they have only a 5 per cent chance of lasting a year without returning to smoking.

2. Nicotine addiction is caused by changes in the reward or pleasure centres of the smoker's brain. Although individual variations exist, everybody who tries a cigarette is at risk of addiction.

3. Pregnant women are urged to stop smoking in their first trimester using a safe and natural method. The foetus can be harmed with serious consequences for the baby's health and later development.

4. Adolescent users of tobacco are at risk of neurological changes that can lead to addiction and also cognitive and emotional changes.

5. Stoppers who use cannabis are advised to take cannabis in some other form. Otherwise it will be a major risk for a smoking relapse.

2

Nicotine replacement therapy, e-cigarettes and anti-smoking drugs: why you should avoid them

Drug-based or pharmaceutical approaches to stopping smoking are today very common as is becoming the use of e-cigarettes (ECs). Companies argue that these are effective ways of stopping smoking. Smokers are offered nicotine in a manner less risky than inhaling smoke from burning tobacco. Or they are offered a medicine as a method of 'weaning' off smoking, using one drug to stop using another. In the case of ECs, nicotine is delivered as a vapour with flavourings that are often given exotic and appealing names.

The effectiveness of drugs and ECs has been tested in clinical trials, studies in which people volunteer to test new drugs or devices. All new treatments (drugs and medical devices) must go through clinical trials before being approved by the Food and Drugs Administration (FDA) in the US, the European Medicines Agency (EMA), and the Medicines and Healthcare Products Regulatory Agency

(MHRA) in the UK. One would like to imagine that the conclusions reached by these agencies are based on the best information science has to offer. Unfortunately, clinical trials and reports can be cleverly manipulated so that drugs are shown in a positive light.

The area of clinical trials is a minefield. What can appear on the surface to be well-controlled scientific clinical trial may have a dubious pedigree. In order to cross the hurdle of FDA/EMA/MHRA approval, drug companies require positive results from clinical trials that follow rigorous scientific methods. But the influence of commercial interests and the need for industrial income flows within universities can lead to outcomes that are not always ideal. We end up in a situation where the health service and the general public may be given drugs that are ineffective or less effective than drug companies claim. Unfortunately, this situation exists with nicotine replacement therapy (NRT). NRT has been heavily promoted by companies, endorsed by expert committees and university professors, yet the evidence on its real world effectiveness is far from strong. This evidence suggests that it is no better than a placebo or a simple sugar pill.

At first sight, the pharmacy approach to smoking seems a bit nuts. Why would you want to replace one form of an addictive drug with another? You wouldn't help an alcoholic by drip-feeding them alcohol. That would be absolutely crazy. Ditto, heroin or cocaine. The fact is that many of the studies are produced by academics who have known conflicts of interest. They may have received fees by companies in return for running clinical trials.

Nicotine replacement therapy

The most commonly advocated method for reducing the craving and the risk of relapse is to use nicotine replacement medication, heavily promoted by the manufacturers. In spite of its popularity, the majority of independent real-world research shows that it is an ineffective method of stopping smoking. The theory is that NRT provides enough nicotine to the body to lessen the urge to smoke and remove the worst of the nicotine withdrawal effects. Forms of NRT include chewing gum, transdermal patches, nasal spray, inhalers and pills.

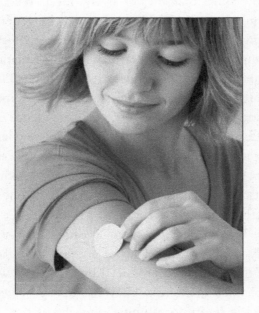

The nicotine patch

The usual source of evidence concerning drugs is clinical trials which often contain conflicts of interest. For instance, a 2004 review by Drs Silagy, Lancaster, Stead, Mant and Fowler reviewed the effectiveness of the different forms of NRT in helping people to stop smoking or in reducing the amount they smoked. The review considered ninety-six randomised trials in which NRT was compared to placebo (no treatment), or where different doses of NRT were compared. The measure used was whether the ex-smokers managed to abstain from smoking for at least six months following treatment compared to a control group of people stopping smoking without NRT. The NRT group were reported to be 1.74 times more likely to abstain than those not using NRT.

The reviewers concluded that all of the commercially available forms of NRT (nicotine gum, transdermal patch, the nicotine nasal spray, nicotine inhaler and nicotine sublingual pills/lozenges) are effective as part of a strategy to stop smoking. They stated that NRT increases stop rates by approximately one-and-a-half to two times. If true, that would be positive proof that NRT is an effective medical approach to stopping smoking. Unfortunately, there are issues with the study (and many others like it) that make such a conclusion highly debatable.

First, there are potential conflicts of interest. Conflicts occur when an author has been paid fees by a sponsor to give advice, carry out a trial, or to speak at conferences. Authors are required by journal policy to state any conflicts that may exist but it is almost impossible to judge how these conflicts may have influenced the study findings. Another trouble with these kinds of controlled clinical studies is the method. The investigators are proud to claim that the study is 'double blind'. In theory, this means that neither the investigators nor the participants know which condition they are in, treatment or control. This prevents biasing the results by expectations and beliefs about the drug effects. The trouble is that the participants may not really be blind and they have ways of telling when they are in the placebo group and they respond differently for this reason.

A third problem with the findings of randomised trials is that the conditions are artificial and the findings from clinical trials rarely hold up in the real world. Evidence from real world studies shows that NRT is ineffective as a method of stopping smoking. An excellent source of information on the scientific literature on real world studies can be found at http://whyquit.com

A Gallup national survey in 2013 found that only one in a hundred successful ex-smokers credited nicotine gum for their success, with only 8 per cent quitting with any approved product, and that more quit smoking cold turkey than by all other methods combined. As early as September 2002, the *Journal of the American Medical Association* reported, 'Since becoming available over the counter, NRT appears no longer effective in increasing long-term successful cessation in California smokers.' This must be true today not only in California but everywhere in the western world.

NRT: yes or no? You need to ask for advice from your doctor and carefully read the information on the package. If you are pregnant or trying to become pregnant, or are breastfeeding, or under the age of 18, smoking fewer than ten cigarettes per day, or have a medical condition, talk to your doctor or advisor before taking NRT medication.

In my opinion, it is best to avoid NRT altogether. If you use CBT to stop smoking, you can make the necessary changes without any need for a nicotine substitute or other medication. Many thousands of my clients have successfully stopped smoking using CBT alone. There is every reason to think that you can do the same. This is actually one of the main benefits of using CBT – it allows you to overcome your smoking habit without the need for medication. I have to be brutally honest with you: the use of NRT is a form of failure. Using NRT proves that you are still addicted to nicotine.

Some stop smoking systems rely a hundred per cent on the continued use of nicotine. If you followed this advice, you could end up wearing patches, chewing gum or vaping nicotine for the rest of your life. That simply isn't viable. It's a stop smoking technique designed for losers. Don't be a loser. Stop smoking now using the process of CBT.

In spite of the risks, adolescent and pregnant smokers have been prescribed NRT by their doctors. Others have acquired it through other means. Some report simultaneous use of NRT and cigarettes. Non-smoking teens have also tried NRT and some have got into the habit of regular use. The easy availability of NRT poses a risk for the curious and adventurous young smokers. Like smoking itself, NRT has the potential of priming the brain for nicotine addiction and it can lead to illegal forms of drug use.

E-cigarettes: cool, cheap and less risky than conventional cigarettes?

The full technical term for e-cigarettes or devices that deliver nicotine is 'electronic nicotine delivery systems' (ENDS). Electronic or e-cigarettes (ECs) mimic normal cigarettes but they deliver nicotine through a vapour. The vapour is produced by battery-powered heating of a solution of chemicals containing nicotine and propylene-glycol. Inhaling the vapour from an EC is called *vaping*. There is no tobacco, no combustion and no smoke. For these reasons, vaping is often viewed as a cool, cheap and less risky alternative to conventional cigarettes.

E-cigarettes fall into three basic types:

1. 'Cigalikes' that resemble tobacco cigarettes, disposable or with pre-filled cartridges;
2. cylindrical 'tanks', designed to be refilled with liquid;
3. larger, rectangular tanks with a large capacity for fluid. Many of the most widely sold brands of cigalikes are now owned by the tobacco industry. Hardly a coincidence!

Intense competition between hundreds of suppliers has created a diverse range of brands, strengths and flavours. Many of the flavours are designed to have special appeal to children and teenagers. They are also technologically quite 'whizzy'. There are ECs that are bluetooth-compatible with Android or iOS devices or tablets, allowing the user to make calls or listen to music while vaping. ECs can even give vapers statistics about their consumption via a mobile app.

The accepted wisdom is that vaping should be less harmful than smoking. This is because it delivers nicotine without the thousands of toxicants in tobacco smoke. ECs do not contain carbon monoxide (CO_2) or many of the other harmful chemicals found in conventional cigarettes. However, because the EC mimics the tobacco cigarette in the mechanics of inhaled delivery of nicotine, it can substitute both for the pharmacologic (nicotine rush) and the behavioural (touch and feel) components of cigarette smoking.

ECs create the 'illusion' of smoking but without any actual smoke. Is this ingenious or dangerous? We can determine now on the basis of current knowledge that ECs are unsafe. There is already sufficient evidence that nicotine is a lethal poison and therefore that ECs are unsafe. Only those with a commercial interest in increasing EC sales would wish to argue otherwise. As stated by the International Programme on Chemical Safety (IPCS): 'Nicotine is one of the most toxic of all poisons and has a rapid onset of action.' There are many different avenues of harm that stem from the EC.

E-cigarettes have been on the market world-wide for a decade and are increasingly popular including among adolescents and pregnant smokers. Yet ECs are unregulated in most countries. Electronic cigarettes are currently the most popular stop smoking aids and evidence indicates they can help people to quit. On the other hand, they can help people to continue smoking also. What is the truth about the e-cigarette?

Currently, there are around 2.5–3 million EC users in the UK. About 10 per cent of US adults vape, according to the online Reuters/Ipsos poll of 5,679 Americans conducted in 2016. This number includes many women who are using ECs during pregnancy and also adolescents. This places unborn children at significant risk and many teenagers may end up with damaged brains. Use of ECs among the young is increasing at exponential rates. This growth in usage is perceived as safe with unregulated advertising geared toward vulnerable populations, such as young women who are likely to smoke or vape during pregnancy.

There is real danger in maternal smoking during pregnancy and the consequences this can have on offspring lung function, including the increased risk of childhood wheezing and subsequent asthma, can be lifelong. Recent evidence strongly suggests that much of this effect is mediated by nicotine, making it highly likely that EC use during pregnancy has the same harmful effects on offspring lung function and health as do conventional cigarettes. In fact, the evidence for nicotine being the mediator of harm of conventional cigarettes may be most compelling for its effects on lung development. This raises concerns about both the combined use of ECs and conventional cigarettes during pregnancy as well as the use of ECs by EC–only users who think them safe or by those sufficiently addicted to nicotine to not be able to quit ECs during pregnancy.

The nicotine vapour inhaled from an EC is produced by the vaporisation of a liquid consisting of nicotine, propylene glycol, glycerine, and flavourings. Liquids are available in 7.2 per cent, and even 10 per cent concentrated solutions of nicotine. The unregulated distribution of e-liquid is a cause for concern. The higher concentrations are available in large quantities on the internet – with sizes ranging from one litre to a gallon for consumer use and up to a fifty-five-gallon drum for manufacturing purposes. A perfect new murder weapon is in the making. Crime writers take note!

The chemicals used to flavour liquids may themselves be quite toxic. There are already at least eight thousand uniquely named flavoured e-liquids, with hundreds of new flavours each month. Makers of e-liquids don't have to list the ingredients and nicotine amounts. The safety of flavourings in the e-liquids has not been evaluated for their risk levels to the lungs.

ECs are sold with chargers. Every few hours the device requires recharging, like a mobile phone. A problem may arise when the user charges the device using the wrong charger. There is a risk that it may actually explode! One man lost part of his tongue and had his teeth blackened. Not surprisingly he gave up vaping immediately. Many such cases have been reported in the media. One unfortunate victim lost an eye during a vaper explosion, leading to litigation.

Nicotine is one of the most toxic of all poisons. Accidental ingestion or absorption of e-liquid from e-cigarettes is increasingly prevalent. The US journal *Pediatrics* reported that in the period January 2012 to April 2015 the US National Poison Data System received 29,141 calls for nicotine and tobacco exposures in children younger than six years. This is an average of 729 child exposures per month. Cigarettes accounted for 60 per cent of exposures, followed by other tobacco products (16 per cent) and ECs (14 per cent). The monthly number of exposures associated with ECs increased by 1492.9 per cent during the study period. One death occurred in association with a nicotine liquid exposure.

The safety information on e-liquid containers is generally inadequate and poorly presented. In many cases, the information is printed in such small print that the warnings are invisible to the naked eye. Candy-flavoured e-liquids are bound to have an instant appeal to children. Flavours such as: Bubble gum, blueberry candy, apple candle, liquorice, butter toffee, blueberry cotton (candy floss). Small wonder hundreds of children are smelling and swallowing these enticing fluids.

The *Pediatrics* authors' report concluded that 'swift government action is needed to regulate these products to help prevent child poisoning. Prevention strategies include public education; appropriate product storage and use away from children; warning labels; and modifications of EC devices, e-liquid, and e-liquid containers and packaging to make them less appealing and less accessible to children.'

There is also at least one reported case of an e-liquid suicide, according to the *Daily Mail* of 28 November 2015.

A hidden danger of ECs is *mislabelling* of the nicotine contents of the e-liquid. People may innocently vape on what appears to be a low dosage of nicotine when, in reality, the level can be much higher. The person would quickly become addicted and switch to conventional cigarette smoking. The *Journal of Pediatric Nursing* reported that only 35 per cent of e-liquid containers were child-resistant. Moreover, more than half of the e-liquid containers were mislabelled by at least 10 per cent. Again, these findings make a strong case for legislation on child-safe packaging and clear nicotine labelling.

Scientific evidence on the safety of the e-cigarette

Until recently, scientific evidence regarding the human health effects of e-cigarettes has been limited. However, studies on EC use are rapidly proliferating. One of the main issues is the vapour itself, the aerosol that is inhaled. While

EC aerosol contains fewer toxicants than cigarette smoke, studies evaluating whether e-cigarettes are less harmful than cigarettes are inconclusive. Some evidence suggests that EC use may facilitate smoking cessation, but definitive data are lacking. No EC has been approved by the FDA as an aid to stopping smoking. Environmental concerns and issues regarding non-user exposure exist. The health impact of ECs, for users and the public, cannot be determined with currently available data.

Has this situation changed in recent years? Yes, it most certainly has. There have been many new studies and the new evidence is not looking good for the EC. The elimination of cigarettes and other combustible tobacco products can prevent tens of millions of tobacco-related deaths. The introduction of ECs could be an important step towards the elimination of the scourge of smoking. However, there is one drawback (if you'll pardon the pun!). Nicotine itself is not harmless. Nicotine exposure can itself do harm, especially during periods of developmental vulnerability such as the foetal through adolescent stages. There can be multiple adverse consequences to early nicotine exposure including impaired development and altered development of the cerebral cortex and hippocampus in adolescents.

Recent legislation

ECs are marketed as smoking cessation aids or as a tobacco replacement. Cancer and respiratory experts see the same ploys being used today with ECs as occurred in the 1940s with cigarettes, when the western world started smoking en masse. Vapourisers are often distributed for free and pitched by celebrities and even doctors as cool, liberating and safe. However, they are not approved in Canada and in a few other countries. In March 2009, Health Canada issued an advisory notice to Canadians not to use ECs as 'These products may pose health risks and have not been fully evaluated for safety, quality and efficacy by Health Canada.' Health Canada said that all electronic products intended to administer inhaled doses of nicotine are considered to be new drugs.

From 2016 new laws in the UK standardised plain packaging on vaping products and made the products weaker. The new rules also specified smaller containers, health warnings, child-proof and tamper-proof e-liquid cartridges and ensured that EC companies would no longer be able to make claims about vaping being beneficial to people's health.

E-cigarettes as a gateway to traditional smoking for adolescents

One effect of the unregulated distribution of e-cigarettes is that it is 're-normalising' smoking. Increasing adolescent EC-use encourages use of traditional cigarettes and dual use, a transition to cigarette use following use of ECs. E-cigarettes acting as a gateway to conventional tobacco smoking is something that adolescents and young adults perceive themselves, according to a Swiss study.

One study used questionnaires in 2014 from eleventh and twelfth grade students in the Southern California Children's Health Study. Among those who had never used cigarettes, 32 per cent of past EC-users and 35 per cent of current EC users indicated susceptibility to cigarette use, compared with 21 per cent of those who had never been EC-users. Susceptibility to cigarette use was reportedly two times higher for current EC-users compared with never users. Unsurprisingly, a social environment that is favourable to ECs is associated with greater susceptibility to cigarette use.

Dual use of e-cigarettes and conventional cigarettes

Using ECs can be the first stepping stone to cigarettes. A second is dual usage. One study among cigarette 'experimenters' (those who have taken at least one puff) found that EC-use was associated with higher odds of cigarette smoking. The researchers concluded that 'use of ECs does not discourage, and may encourage, conventional cigarette use among US adolescents.'

Another study examined the association between the type of EC used, frequency of use and quitting. An online survey included 1,643 current smokers, 64 per cent of whom reported no EC use, 27 per cent used cigalikes, and 9 per cent used tanks. The results suggested that 'tinkering' with EC-use gives the smoker a lower chance of stopping smoking.

Dual use of e-cigarettes with NRT

Drs. Farsalinos, Romagna and Voudris examined factors associated with dual use of tobacco and electronic cigarettes with 7,060 EC-users. They found that risk perception is a good indicator of dual use. Dual users had a longer smoking history and a lower daily consumption of cigarettes. Their daily consumption of tobacco cigarettes declined from twenty to four cigarettes a day after using ECs. Most of the users were daily vapers but many were using their electronic cigarette occasionally compared to full-time vapers. The most convincing indicators of dual use were: a higher risk perception among vapers; the use of first generations of devices; the use of pre-filled cartomisers; the occasional use of ECs. The results of this study show that higher risk perception and less frequent use of ECs are associated with the dual use of electronic and tobacco cigarettes.

E-cigarettes as carriers for drugs more potent than nicotine

E-cigarettes open doors to drug use beyond nicotine. They can be used with all kinds of fluids and mixtures apart from e-liquid – for example, marijuana. Researchers surveyed 3,847 Connecticut high-school students and found nearly one in five EC users also used the device to vaporise cannabis or by-products like hash oil, which can also be substituted for the nicotine solution in many traditional ECs. Some vendors sell ECs specifically designed for marijuana leaves or wax infused with THC, the active ingredient in marijuana. Vaping concentrated liquid forms of marijuana can be much more potent than smoking dried marijuana leaves.

Drug users have discovered a method of adapting ECs to vaporise a potent class of hallucinogen known as dimethyl-tryptamine, or DMT. This hack is discussed openly on web forums, with DMT enthusiasts describing how simple it is to consume the drug using an EC. Although modifying an EC in preparation for smoking DMT is relatively simple, errors can prove dangerous. Reports have surfaced online of people claiming to have felt a burning sensation on their lungs while attempting to smoke the drug in this manner. Not a good idea!

E-cigarettes as a tool for long-term smoking cessation

The World Health Organization (WHO) has banned therapeutic claims by manufacturers of ECs. One study looked at ECs and smoking cessation in real-world and clinical settings. Because smokers are increasingly using ECs for many reasons, including attempts to quit combustible cigarettes and to use nicotine where smoking is prohibited, the investigators aimed to assess the association between EC use and cigarette-smoking cessation among adults, irre-spective of their motivation for using ECs. They said that the odds of quitting cigarettes were 28 per cent lower in those who used ECs compared with those who did not use e-cigarettes. The authors concluded, 'As currently being used, ECs are associated with significantly less quitting among smokers.'

So much for the hype about e-cigarettes helping smokers to quit. The evidence suggests the opposite is the case.

E-cigarette marketing

Promotional spending is rapidly increasing. Levels of TV advertising are increasing as tobacco companies acquire an increasing share of the market. EC marketers are applying advertising ideas from the tobacco industry, allowing products to be marketed to promote traditional smoking. A key reason for the success of EC marketing is the proposition that they are safer than conventional cigarettes. A study tested whether receptivity to EC marketing is associated with recent EC use among young adults through increased beliefs that ECs are less harmful than cigarettes. The findings suggest that marketing of ECs as safer alternatives to cigarettes or cessation aids is associated with increased EC use among young adults.

Researchers assessed adult smokers' exposure to information about e-cigarettes, asking whether or not their exposure predicted EC use behaviour and perceptions about addiction and reduced harm and the role then played by reduced harm perceptions. Forty per cent of 2,254 people reported seeing, hearing, or reading about EC in the media 'a lot of times', with TV and point-of-sale being the most common channels of exposure. Those reporting a lot of exposure were 40 per cent more likely than those reporting low or no exposure to say that using ECs was 'not at all harmful' to a person's health and 40 per cent more likely to say they use ECs every day or some days. These results suggest that exposure to information about EC is associated with reduced harm perceptions and greater use.

E-cigarettes are marketed over all forms media, including sports and cultural sponsorship, celebrity endorsement, social networking, online advertising and through pricing strategies and product innovation. ECs are being sold as a product for hipsters, the same image that was used in tobacco advertising. The EC user is modelled as independent, making a lifestyle choice, identifying with celebrities and being seen at fashionable, trendy places and taking part in activities. As the WHO report correctly noted, some ECs are marketed as socially superior to conventional cigarettes. However, 'unsubstantiated or overstated claims of safety and cessation are frequent marketing themes aimed at smokers. Some EC marketing also promotes long-term use as a permanent alternative to tobacco and a temporary one in public places where smoking is banned.'

Glamorising smoking and attracting children and non-smokers is all part of the message. The use of candy-like flavours in the marketing such is likely to entice children or teenagers to experiment with ECs. It is, of course, in the interests of the industry that the EC remains unregulated, that so-called experts state that the safety is unknown and will not be known for decades. The truth is that we know now that ECs are unsafe.

Physical, cognitive and mood effects

The most commonly used reasons for vaping is that ECs aid quitting, help avoid relapse, reduce the urge to smoke and form a lower risk alternative to traditional smoking. How much nicotine does vaping put into the blood? Does it have the expected effects on urges and craving? A study examined the effect of using an 18 mg/ml nicotine first generation EC on blood nicotine, tobacco withdrawal symptoms and urge to smoke.

Three female and eleven male regular EC users who had been abstinent from smoking and EC use for twelve hours completed a three-hour testing session. Blood was sampled and questionnaires completed concerning their tobacco-related withdrawal symptoms, urge to smoke, positive and negative subjective effects at four stages: baseline, ten puffs, sixty minutes of ad lib use and a sixty-minute rest period. Complete sets of blood were obtained from seven participants (that's a bit odd – what happened to the other seven?). Blood nicotine concentration rose significantly across those stages. The authors concluded that tobacco-related withdrawal symptoms and the urge-to-smoke were significantly reduced. Direct positive effects were strongly endorsed and there were few reports of any adverse effects. They also clearly showed that reliable blood nicotine delivery does indeed occur after acute use of this brand of EC in a sample of regular users. Hardly surprising I guess. It's a bit like asking whether drinking whisky puts alcohol into your bloodstream and gets you drunk?

Anti-smoking medication: why you should avoid it

Bupropion

Bupropion, also known as Zyban and Wellbutrin, is a nicotine-free treatment licensed for smoking cessation. It is claimed that Bupropion helps to reduce nicotine withdrawal and the urge to smoke. Bupropion can be used safely with NRT, the company literature states.

An issue to be aware of, if you are contemplating using Zyban, is the possibility of side effects. The most common side effects are a dry mouth, insomnia, a change in appetite, agitation and headaches. The most common side effects which cause people to discontinue use of bupropion are shakiness and skin rash. Also, bupropion can cause seizures. If you have epilepsy or an existing seizure disorder, you definitely should not take this drug. It is also important to carefully follow your doctor's recommendations about dosage, due to the risk of seizures.

Guidance to doctors on Zyban

Soon after the introduction of Zyban as a prescription drug, newspapers began reporting deaths in patients prescribed with Zyban. *The Guardian* reported in 2001 that the anti-smoking drug was suspected of causing adverse reactions in thirty-five people who had died in the UK since it was introduced in June 2000. This acknowledgement came at the inquest of Kerry Weston, aged twenty-one, a British Airways air hostess who was found dead in a hotel room in

Nairobi, Kenya, two weeks after she began taking the drug to help her quit her fifteen-a-day habit.

Following these reports, in May 2001 the Committee on Safety of Medicines (CSM) announced a change to the prescribing regime and strengthened warnings for doctors prescribing Zyban. The CSM reviewed current evidence and advised a delay in increasing the dosage during the period of treatment and a strengthening of the warnings given to prescribers that Zyban should only be used for patients at risk for seizures if there were compelling clinical reasons.

Professor Breckenridge, Chair of the CSM said:

> 'The Committee on Safety of Medicines and the Medicines Control Agency in conjunction with other European regulatory authorities ... will be keeping the safety of Zyban under close, constant scrutiny.'

Suicide risk

Two investigators in Finland, Dr Pirkko Kriikku and Dr Ilkka Ojanperä investigated the relationship between bupropion and suicide in post-mortem investigations (in *Forensic Science International*, 23 June 2016). They reviewed 33,727 post-mortem investigations in Finland from 2009–2013 and identified cases in which bupropion was detected. Cases positive for other antidepressant drugs were reviewed for comparison.

The post-mortem examinations included, in all cases, the routine screening and quantification of hundreds of drugs and poisons. Bupropion was detected in sixty-five cases. While this is only .2 per cent of all deaths, a large proportion of the bupropion–positive deaths resulted from suicide (55 per cent). In fatal poisoning cases found positive for bupropion, the proportion of suicide was even higher (77 per cent).

The research 'highlights' were:

- Suicide was the most common manner of death among users of bupropion.
- Suicide was significantly more common among users of bupropion than among users of other antidepressant drugs.
- Individuals positive for bupropion died younger than users of other antidepressants.

There are no known suicides following the use of CBT to stop smoking. CBT is definitely a safer option than bupropion.

Smiling is not the only reaction to anti-smoking medications. Users have experienced adverse reactions.

Varenicline

Also known under the trade names of Chantix or Champix, varenicline is a medicine licensed in the US and UK in 2006. It is claimed that varenicline mimics the effect of nicotine on the body. Varenicline is a nicotinic receptor partial agonist – it stimulates nicotine receptors more weakly than nicotine. Therefore, it can reduce the urge to smoke and relieve withdrawal symptoms. The normal dosage is 1 mg twice daily for twelve weeks. Varenicline has not been tested in those under eighteen or pregnant women and therefore is not recommended for use by these groups.

In 2009 the FDA announced a 'black box' warning – its most serious alert – on the prescribing information for Chantix (varenicline) and Zyban (bupropion). The warning highlighted the risk of serious mental health events including changes in behaviour, depressed mood, hostility, and suicidal thoughts when taking these drugs. 'The risk of serious adverse events while taking these products must be weighed against the significant health benefits of quitting smoking,' said Dr Janet Woodcock, the director of the FDA's Center for Drug Evaluation and Research. 'Smoking is the leading cause of preventable disease, disability, and death in the USA and we know these products are effective aids in helping people quit.'

The FDA also issued a warning that Chantix 'may be associated with a small, increased risk of certain cardiovascular adverse events in patients who have cardiovascular disease'.

Side effects of the drug include nausea in approximately 30 per cent of people taking varenicline, headaches, insomnia, and nightmares. More rarely occurring side effects include change in taste, vomiting, abdominal pain, flatulence, and constipation. Aljazeera America reported that, over five years, 544 suicides and 1,869 attempted suicides had been reported to the FDA as 'adverse events' in connection with Chantix, according to documents obtained under the Freedom of Information Act. The FDA asked pharmaceutical giant Pfizer to investigate reports of violence by Chantix users.

You need to ask yourself whether the chance to stop smoking using a medicine like Chantix or Champix is worth the risk. A vitally interesting scientific report was published in 2016. This was the largest clinical trial on anti-smoking medication ever conducted.

The FDA and Big Pharma clinical trial

Many deaths have been reported in the media and elsewhere following smokers' usage of bupropion and varenicline. However, it is difficult to absolutely prove these deaths were caused by the drugs. It is true that the suicide data from Finland are quite convincing. Sixty-five buproprion-linked suicides in Finland and 2,700 lawsuits in America are difficult to ignore. However, there could be additional factors other than the drug itself that led to the deaths; e.g. drug abuse, alcohol abuse, depression, family issues, unemployment and stress. To establish cause and effect it is necessary to carry out a controlled trial.

Following the theory that there's no smoke without fire, the FDA requested a trial to investigate the association between the anti-smoking medications and psychiatric disorders. The study was reported in *The Lancet* in 2016 by Robert Anthenelli and colleagues. The investigators included several known advocates of anti-smoking medications working in collaboration with company scientists from Pfizer and GlaxoSmithKline, the funders of the study.

Incredible though it might seem, the investigators administered the drugs to 8,144 people, half of whom had a history of psychiatric problems. The study sample included 3,549 (44 per cent) men, who had an average age of forty-six and a half years, and 6,584 (82 per cent) participants who were of white race. The aim was to measure the incidence of moderate and severe adverse events.

It is important to note that, 'Participants had to be considered clinically stable for inclusion (i.e., no exacerbations of their condition in the preceding six months; on stable treatment for at least three months, with no treatment change anticipated during the study) and considered by the investigator not to be at high risk of self-injury or suicidal behaviour.' The participants were given either varenicline (1 mg twice daily) or bupropion (150 mg twice daily) or a nicotine patch (21 mg per day) or a placebo for twelve weeks with a twelve-week non-treatment follow-up. What did they find?

First the good news: nobody died! Daily visits and close supervision from the researchers made that an impossibility. All three of the anti-smoking medications produced reductions in smoking. Varenicline produced the strongest effect, doubling the abstinence rates for buproprion and NRT patch.

Now the bad news. Considering only the non-psychiatric sample, all three of the medications led to significant increases in psychiatric symptoms. Approximately one in three of the bupropion group showed signs of psychiatric disorder – a statistically higher number than in the placebo group. This result was only possible through chance with a probability of one in ten thousand. The varenicline group and the nicotine patch group also showed significantly higher rates of psychiatric disorders. Of particular significance was the increased incidence of abnormal dreams and insomnia. In addition, a quarter of the varenicline group experienced nausea.

It is impossible to know what aspects of the results of this highly controlled trial would be repeated in the real world. We do know that real world studies never produce the same high abstinence rates obtained in clinical trials. We also do not know the full impact of bupropion and varenicline when combined with recreational use of alcohol and illicit drugs, something that can easily happen in the everyday, real world. However, there are plenty of scary reports in the media. The FDA issued a drug safety communication in the USA in 2011 that included potential alcohol interaction, risk of seizures and studies of side effects on mood, behaviour or thinking.

In 2015 the FDA announced that a moderate-level drug interaction exists between varenicline and alcohol; some patients have experienced decreased tolerance to alcohol, including increased drunkenness, unusual or aggressive behaviour or they were unable to recall events. Users have been advised to limit their consumption of alcohol until they know whether or not it affects their tolerance. Also they have been advised to use caution driving or operating machinery until they know how quitting smoking and/or varenicline may affect them.

If a varenicline user develops nervousness, agitation or hostility or shows signs of aggressive behaviour, depression, thoughts of suicide or has other changes in behaviour or thinking that are not typical, the FDA warns that they must immediately stop taking varenicline and contact their doctor.

A moderate-level drug interaction also occurs when using nicotine together with varenicline, something which can cause an increase in side effects. There is a long list of medications not to be used with varenicline, including all forms of NRT.

Conclusions

1. Real world studies of NRT consistently show that NRT is no more effective than a placebo.
2. Another alternative is the EC, branded as a cheap, cool and less risky alternative to the conventional cigarette. They may well be cheaper and even 'cooler' perhaps, but they are certainly not risk-free and certainly not safe.
3. There is no way of escaping the fact that nicotine is a lethal poison. Lack of safety of ECs and e-liquids is a major issue. Many poisonings are occurring as

infants and children are drinking e-liquids directly out of the bottle.

4. The EC can be a stepping stone to conventional cigarette use, which leads to dual use, then to conventional smoking and possibly to abuse of other drugs.

5. Smokers who switch to ECs must remain addicted to nicotine. There is no convincing evidence that ECs do actually help smokers to quit.

6. Medication is unsafe. You can ask yourself whether you wish to rely on a drug that has a high chance of giving you nausea, sleepless nights, bad dreams and maybe worse. My recommendation is to steer clear of anti-smoking medications.

7. A far better solution is to stop smoking with CBT and mindfulness. CBT and meditation are both more effective and safer than medication.

3

How cognitive behavioural therapy can help you to stop smoking now

General principles

In this section I present a brief introduction to the methods used in *Stop Smoking Now*. Probably, you have tried to stop smoking many times before. You know how hard it can be. Most people have to try several times before finally being able to stop. In the previous chapter we saw what a powerfully addictive drug nicotine really is, more addictive than heroin or cocaine.

In the past, each time that you tried to stop smoking, even though you did not succeed, your efforts were not entirely wasted. You learned something, some insights into what helps you and what hinders you. That knowledge will help you to stop smoking now.

Stop Smoking Now is based on cognitive behavioural therapy (CBT) and mindfulness-based cognitive therapy. The key principles are that you live in the present and become aware of your smoking experiences. From a present-centred awareness of your smoking you can learn how to control it. This is the best possible preparation for your first step on the seven-step ladder described below.

1. Getting support.
2. Removing the reward value and pleasure of smoking.
3. Identifying and learning not to respond to smoking triggers.
4. Removing the craving and stress-smoke spiral.
5. Becoming mindful of smoking/non-smoking experience.
6. Preparing for relapse or difficult situations.

You have the best chances if you progress along each of these steps in turn. *Stop Smoking Now* will give you everything you need to move through these stages. The traditional methods of stopping smoking advocate the use of strong willpower combined with medication. CBT combined with mindfulness offers you a more advanced and effective approach. It is simple, free, harmless, powerful, and natural. You will be using the power of the mind to heal itself by controlling your behaviour and changing your experience of pleasure that you gain from smoking. You will be much less reliant on willpower and drugs, both of which have severe drawbacks.

Willpower is often not available in sufficient amounts to make the changes that you desire. Most smokers feel too weak-willed to stop smoking without other means of help. As a consequence, this may lead to a visit to the doctor, who will give you medication. To an increasing extent these days, smoking is being treated using drug therapy alone, when a more powerful and natural approach is available using CBT with mindfulness.

Drugs may temporarily ease the cravings and urges that prompt smoking and they may substitute for the nicotine itself. However, substituting one form of nicotine with another is not a cure. None of the psychological triggers that lead to smoking are removed by drug therapy; as soon as the nicotine replacement therapy (NRT) is no longer available, the triggers will pull you back to cigarettes. Drugs also have unwanted side effects and may be as addictive as tobacco itself. There is certainly no point in replacing one addiction with another. Medication, if used wisely, can be extremely beneficial. But it works best in combination with techniques that allow you to modify your behaviour: in other words, CBT.

In the UK, the NHS has not yet adopted CBT for patients who smoke. The UK Department of Health advocates CBT for treatment of anxiety and depression, eating disorders and obesity. Yet, strangely, the department adopted the traditional medical model of NRT and other drugs such as Zyban as a treatment for smokers.

The medical model is a poor performer when it comes to human behaviour. Smoking is an activity with physical and psychological aspects. Drugs can, to some degree, address the physical aspects of smoking, but they cannot change the psychological aspects. The results from the NHS system of stopping smoking are disappointing. No objective data have been published on the actual abstinence rates, validated by biochemical markers, either short-term or long-term. All the statistics show is how many people said that they had stopped at four weeks: less than half.

What is CBT?

CBT uses the natural power of the mind to heal and restore by modifying excessive and unhealthy behaviours and feelings. Mental processes can change behaviour, thoughts and feelings by setting new goals and plans. CBT is safe, effective, and natural. Without any doubt, CBT is the best and safest method of stopping smoking available today. You can use it if you are female or male, pregnant, young or old, regardless of your religious beliefs, culture, sexual orientation or disabilities. It is a universally applicable method that uses the power of your mind and brain to change.

The human mind-brain is infinitely flexible. We are lucky – very, very lucky! You have within you the power to change. Now is the time to use that power. Without drugs, or hypnosis, or any form of hocus–pocus, you have the ability to change, by yourself, with a little help from CBT.

The mind consists of thoughts, emotions and behaviour. These processes all affect one another and make you do whatever you choose to do. CBT is a system for changing these processes. When we change these processes, we are also changing the activity of the brain. The networks in the brain of a smoker have been altered by the addiction to nicotine. The brain is programmed, like a computer, to accept the addiction. With the toolbox of CBT we are able to bring the brain back to its non-addicted state. The relationships between thoughts, emotions, behaviour and the brain form the Brain Pyramid.

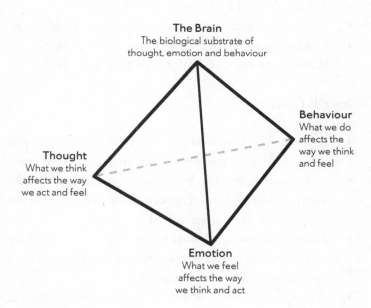

The Brain
The biological substrate of
thought, emotion and behaviour

Behaviour
What we do
affects the
way we think
and feel

Thought
What we think
affects the way
we act and feel

Emotion
What we feel
affects the way
we think and act

The Brain Pyramid.

I describe in later chapters exactly how the different parts of the brain are involved in your addiction.

CBT is a system of change. CBT will enable you to:

- Change your thinking and beliefs about smoking.
- Reduce the pleasure and reward value of smoking.
- Monitor your smoking behaviour, so you understand when and why it happens.
- Help prevent you from responding to smoking triggers.
- Learn new skills and behaviours to bring about change.
- Take you off the 'stress-smoke spiral'.
- Control smoking with no or minimum use of drugs.
- Control smoking with minimum use of willpower.
- Return to a normal, healthy, happy nicotine-free life.

What CBT is not:

- A form of brain-washing. You do it because you want to do it. It can never happen against your will.
- A form of hypnosis. You carry out CBT in a fully alert, awake state of consciousness. You are in no sense of the term 'hypnotised'.
- A form of magic. Although the effects can be very impressive, it is not magic, but a natural method of controlling your own behaviour.
- A way of increasing your willpower. Your willpower will not be affected by CBT. You will need to use less willpower, but CBT does not increase it.
- A way of controlling the environment. It is you that will change, and the way that you react to the environment, not the environment itself.

Why isn't willpower enough?

The main reason willpower is not enough is that it is extremely difficult to break an addiction purely because you want to. It doesn't matter how much you try to force yourself to stop smoking because your addiction is a physiological state, similar to hunger. The longer you leave it, the worse it gets. Cravings for nicotine, when you have been unable to smoke for a while, are similar to cravings for food when you're hungry or for water when you are thirsty. The nicotine addiction has created a new bodily need. The root cause of the cravings is so persistent that it requires powerful psychological techniques that have been especially developed to change habits and addictions.

Each and every occasion that you have a smoke is a separate smoking habit. Each set of circumstances in which you smoke contains at least one 'trigger' that sets a whole chain of activity moving. You have learned these chains of behaviour over several months or years. Now you need a system for breaking away from your smoking chains, for reversing the habits formed over a long time. Over the page is a typical smoking chain, which is repeated each and every time that you smoke.

Another reason willpower is not enough is that the body and mind are never fixed in one stable state. They are in a constant flux of energy and activity as the individual responds to the changing environment. When demands are high, the body/mind may lack sufficient resources to deal with these demands. This state is what we refer to as 'stress'. The smoker always responds to stress in one

1	Reach for packet
2	Hold packet in one hand
3	Remove one cigarette
4	Place cigarette in mouth
5	Find lighter or matches
6	Light cigarette
7	Inhale first puff
8	Exhale first puff
9	Place cigarette in ashtray
10	Pick up cigarette from ashtray
11	Inhale second puff
12	Exhale second puff
13–30	Another nine or more puffs
31	Put down cigarette
32	Stub cigarette out

way, by smoking. This creates a 'stress-smoke spiral': the stress, or what psychologists call 'negative affect', triggers smoking and smoking triggers more stress. The two things serve as triggers for each other, creating a self-perpetuating spiral. It is difficult to escape the spiral without a powerful intervention.

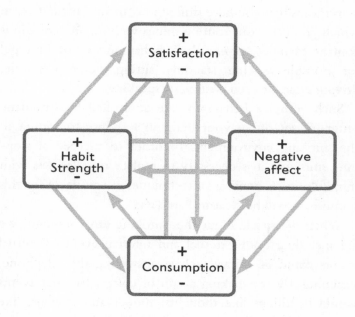

The Stress-Smoke Spiral.

Automatic programs

Another way of understanding smoking behaviour is to look at the automatic 'programs' in your brain that control your everyday activities. I use the American spelling of 'programs' here because it is the connotation of 'computer programs' that I want to indicate. Your smoking behaviour is a chain of events that has a trigger, quite often without any conscious awareness on your part. Much of the time, you can smoke without even being totally aware of what you are doing. Psychologists refer to this as 'mindlessness'. This means that you have drifted into an automatic state, in which you carry out routine things without any conscious control. Many of our most basic behaviours are of this type, for example walking, standing, sitting, riding a bicycle, driving a car, or even writing or speaking.

Such complex behaviours are controlled by automatic programs set off in your brain in response to stimuli in the smoking environment. In order to succeed at stopping smoking, it is necessary to replace mindlessness with mindfulness. A number of techniques are available for this purpose, as will be clear in Part Two.

When we speak about the 'smoking environment', we are including both external and internal events. External events could be things such as answering the telephone, watching TV, or making a cup of coffee. Internal events would be things like thoughts, moods and feelings, like feeling bored, feeling stressed, or thinking about a problem. All of the things that you normally do or think or feel when you smoke are part of the 'smoking environment'.

Some stop smoking 'experts' tell you that to stop smoking, you need to avoid all the aspects of the smoking environment that are associated with smoking. Well, that's just crazy. You would almost have to stop everything that you normally do. What kind of a life would you have if you followed that advice? No, that's no way to carry on. You need to carry on doing all of the things that you normally do, but without the smoking. *Stop Smoking Now* shows you how to do that.

Automatic routines are a very important part of everyday living. We all have many routines that we carry out daily. Some are very ordinary things, like walking, talking or doing the dishes. Other things can be quite specialised, such as using a computer to do word processing or to send an email. Those who become experts in particular skills learn to carry out complicated activities without needing to use any conscious planning or control, for example painting, playing the piano, conducting an orchestra, swinging a golf club or swerving a ball into a goal.

The better learned the behaviour, the more automatic it becomes. Think about learning to ride a bicycle. At first the rider can hardly even sit on the saddle without falling off. Every move has to be consciously planned and decided. Then, if somebody supports and guides the bike, while the rider puts their feet on the pedals and starts to pedal, it will be possible to ride the bicycle without falling off. Eventually, the novice can learn to pedal and control the bicycle and stay balanced without any external help. Then, with more practice, he or she can learn to ride the bike smoothly without thinking about each separate action.

A similar process is involved in learning to smoke. At first the novice will find it a very unpleasant and difficult process. The smoke tastes toxic and hot and the initiate will probably feel sweaty and notice their pulse racing, perhaps even feeling palpitations. The natural tendency is to cough and choke on the fumes of the tobacco and it takes a considerable amount of focused attention to continue the puffing activity. With perseverance, the novice can begin to inhale the smoke without coughing. It happens more and more automatically. Nicotine directly affects the brain and, during the first few cigarettes, the reward, reinforcement and addiction processes begin to kick in. The smoker soon becomes tolerant of the unpleasant sensations in their mouth and throat and cigarettes can be smoked without even noticing unpleasant physiological effects. Eventually, it is satisfying to smoke because the addiction has become stronger and the smoker needs a fix of nicotine to maintain the level of nicotine in the body above a certain level.

Perhaps you can remember your own first cigarette. Can you honestly say that you enjoyed it? If you are honest with yourself, you will probably admit that you hated every second of it. Often the novice is initiated into smoking with a friend or two. It's almost a rite of passage. The initiate puts on the bravest of faces while, deep down, longing for the cigarette to be finished and stubbed out. However, this bravado doesn't need to continue for very long. Nicotine takes over and, before long, a person becomes its slave, with nicotine-controlled smoking chains, triggers and automatic programs ruling their behaviour. Another nicotine slave is born.

Evidence that CBT can help you stop smoking

Smoking is the most addictive and dangerous habit that any human can ever acquire. It is also the most difficult habit to overcome. Rarely can a smoker successfully overcome the habit simply by using power of will. It takes a lot of skill and dogged perseverance as well as sheer hard work. The smoker requires skills and techniques that he or she can have real confidence in. Psychology has a lot to offer in the form of theory, research and practice about behaviour change. Smoking is very stubborn behaviour to change, but it can be changed if the right principles are adopted. Turning to a shotgun drug method is absolutely a last resort, if not an actual sign of defeat.

CBT has been thoroughly tried and tested, not only in the field of smoking but with all kinds of behaviours and experiences. In fact, any behaviour that a person wants to change is amenable to CBT. CBT has been tried in various forms by tens of thousands of smokers with results that are among the best on record. Independent research found that 82 per cent of participants stopped smoking for one day or more by the end of the one-week programme. Thirty-nine per cent were still not smoking one year after attending the programme. This is the highest success rate from a smoking cessation programme ever recorded.

CBT puts the control of smoking into your hands. The CBT tools in Part Two help you to explore your smoking environment for the triggers, the partly hidden signals and motives that affect your smoking behaviour. I already mentioned the great benefit of focusing on the present. This is a wonderfully natural way of being, becoming aware of your conscious experiences, a teachable moment to explore and experiment with. If you are open to learning about yourself and the habits that keep you smoking, you can quickly learn to shake off your mental shackles and become free. Please try all of the *Stop Smoking Now* methods. Your chances of success are increased with the number of methods you choose to employ.

In Part Two, I show you how to reduce your cigarette consumption each day until it reaches zero. Using a present-centred approach, you will learn how to keep any discomfort down to the minimum. After successfully completing your Stop-Day, you will be ready for Part Three, where you'll work at maintaining non-smoking on a permanent basis. Before you begin using the programme, it will be helpful to understand the basics of CBT and mindfulness.

Thought and feeling

CBT emphasises the important role of thinking in everything we feel and do. It is our thinking that causes us to feel and act the way we do. Therefore, if we are experiencing unwanted feelings and behaviours, it is important to identify the thinking that is causing the feelings and behaviours and to learn how to replace this thinking with thoughts that lead to more desirable reactions.

This idea goes way back to classic philosophy. Shakespeare's Hamlet said, 'For there is nothing either good or bad, but thinking makes it so. To Hamlet, the country of Denmark felt like a prison. He said he could live in a walnut but not in Denmark. From these words in Hamlet, we can infer that Shakespeare was thinking like a modern-day cognitive behavioural therapist.

The idea that goodness or happiness are mental concepts is illustrated by the Buddhist story of the farmer and the horse:

One day in late summer, an old farmer was working in his field with his old sick horse. The farmer felt compassion for the horse and desired to lift its burden. So he left his horse loose to go the mountains and live out the rest of its life.

Soon after, neighbours from the nearby village visited, offering their condolences and said, 'What a shame. Now your only horse is gone. How unfortunate you are! You must be very sad. How will you live, work the land, and prosper?'

The farmer replied, 'Who knows? We shall see.'

Two days later the old horse came back, now rejuvenated after meandering on the mountainside while eating the wild grasses. He came back with twelve new younger and healthy horses that followed the old horse into the corral. Word got out in the village of the old farmer's good fortune and it wasn't long before people stopped by to congratulate the farmer on his good luck.

'How fortunate you are!' they exclaimed. 'You must be very happy!'

Again, the farmer softly said, 'Who knows? We shall see.'

At daybreak on the next morning, the farmer's only son set off to attempt to train the new wild horses, but the was thrown to the ground and broke his leg. One by one villagers arrived during the day to bemoan the farmer's misfortune. 'Oh, what a tragedy! Your son won't be able to help you farm with a broken leg. You'll have to do all the work yourself, how will you survive? You must be very sad?' they said. Calmly going about his usual business the farmer answered, 'Who knows? We shall see.'

Several days later a war broke out. The Emperor's men arrived in the village demanding that young men come with them to be conscripted into the Emperor's army. As it happened, the farmer's son was deemed unfit because of his broken leg. 'What very good fortune you have!' the villagers exclaimed as their own young sons were marched away. 'You must be very happy?'

'Who knows? We shall see.' replied the farmer as he headed off to work his field alone.

As time went on, the son's broken leg healed but he was left with a slight limp. Again the neighbours came to pay their condolences. 'Oh, what bad luck. Too bad for you!' But the old farmer simply replied, 'Who knows? We shall see.'

As it turned out the other young village boys had died in the war and the old farmer and his son were the only able-bodied men capable of working the village lands. The old farmer became wealthy and was very generous to the villagers. They said, 'Oh, how fortunate you are – you must be very happy?' to which the old farmer replied, 'Who knows? We shall see.'

Principles of CBT

1. CBT assumes that thinking causes our actions and emotional responses

If you can change the way you think, you can change the way you feel and act, even when the environment remains the same. How much would you give to escape from your prison that is smoking? Are you willing to give it a whirl? You've got everything to gain and nothing to lose. Go for it!

2. CBT is time-limited

CBT is brief. It uses a self-discovery method and makes use of 'homework' assignments and exercises.

3. CBT is a collaboration between the author and the reader

The author and the reader are a team. I suggest ideas for you to try out and you will see what works and what doesn't work. We are in this together! Every person is unique. You will adapt and create the best ways in which to apply the methods I suggest to you in your own way. There are no formulas. Only guiding principles that you will tailor to your own specific needs and niches.

4. CBT is based on changing your thoughts and actions

CBT will help you to explore and understand how your thoughts and actions influence each other. It will show you can learn to do both differently. CBT helps to show you the benefits of jumping off the stress–smoke spiral by learning how to feel calm when confronted with undesirable stress. This could also be helpful outside of the issue of smoking.

5. CBT uses self-questioning

CBT encourages you to ask questions of yourself, for example, 'I feel like a smoke every time I have a cup of coffee. How can I stop doing that?'

6. CBT is structured and directive

CBT gives you new techniques every day. Specific techniques and concepts are illustrated for each day until you stop smoking. CBT focuses on the goals you will set. CBT is directive towards goals. CBT tells you *what* would be good to do and *how* to do it. You will be the one who decides *how, when* and *where* you will do things, smoke or not smoke, under the guidance of the CBT methodology.

7. CBT is based on a learning model

CBT is based on the assumption that emotional and behavioural reactions are learned. Therefore, the goal is to help you to *unlearn* unwanted reactions and to learn new ways of reacting. When you understand *how, when* and *where* you are smoking or not smoking, you will be able to change your traditional responses. It makes it easier to change things, once you know the root causes. CBT gives you your 'get out of jail' card.

8. CBT theory and techniques rely on testing theories and making predictions

The method encourages us to test hypotheses about your behaviour to see if they are correct. You become a 'scientist' about yourself and your smoking and learn to test theories and to make predictions. This can be instructive and fun.

9. Homework is a central feature of CBT

If you are going to be successful, you will need to practise the techniques in this book. Are you up for it?

Three main areas of CBT

CBT focuses on three main areas:

1. Cognitive processes – what we think

You will learn methods and ways to change your old thinking patterns and habits. You will train your mind to think and respond differently than you have in the past. There are thirty specific methods and techniques that you will learn to use – and you only need to find several methods that work well for you.

Some effective techniques are:

- Slowing down the smoking process to discover what is going on.
- Stopping automatic negative thinking or rationalisation.
- Learning rational and helpful self-statements that can become permanent and 'automatic'.
- Learning to listen to the voice of the new you – the non-smoker. Whose voice do you want to listen to, anyhow? Do you have to listen and believe all of the old lies told to you by your addicted self?
- Focusing: what are you paying attention to?
- Imagery rehearsal: picturing your new behaviours in the old worn-out situations.
- Self-imaging: who do you want to be? How do you wish to behave? What kind of a person are you becoming?

2. Behavioural processes – what we do

This is the part where we put into place new behaviours and remove old ones. You must do this in everyday, real-life situations, not just in your head. This is where CBT can be so powerful. This area is tackled right from the very beginning of the process of stopping and work continues all the way through to the end.

3. Emotional processes – what we feel

Smoking is an emotion-laden automatic chain of behaviour and experiences. The emotions set the tone for the behaviours. The thoughts set the agenda. It is important to have some type of relaxation or 'de-stress' strategy. Calmness, confidence and peace are the main goals. You must learn to break the stress–smoke spiral.

The quieter and more relaxed you feel as you make the changes, the more easily the therapeutic process can occur. This calmness and peaceful feeling will let the therapy gently take effect and you will in effect make a new beginning. The focus is on healing, healthiness and inner peace.

The only way an effective 'cure' for smoking can be achieved is by operating on all three of these levels. CBT does just that.

Mindfulness-based cognitive therapy

'Mindfulness' has become a buzzword these days and a bit of a fad. When you cut through the hype, in essence, it's very simple. Being mindful is a state of active, open attention to the experiences that are present. When you're being 'mindful', you are observing your actions, thoughts and feelings, as if from a distance, without judging them as good or bad. Mindfulness means living in the present and awakening to your experience now. It is about 'being' as well as 'doing'. To stop smoking, you need to focus on both doing and being.

Mindfulness-based cognitive therapy (MBCT) is an extra ingredient in *Stop Smoking Now* that helps to make it an even more powerful strategy. Mindfulness always was a component of the process, but it's labelled more clearly in this edition. Mindfulness strengthens the idea that your life is something to be lived in the present and the things that you do should not always be judged as necessarily good or bad. Remember, there is nothing either good or bad, but thinking makes it so.

MBCT uses a simple form of meditation that is practised sitting with eyes closed, on a cushion, or on a chair, with the back as straight as possible. We discuss meditation in more detail along with other tools and techniques in Part Two. Meditation is a helpful aspect of *Stop Smoking Now*. One gently focuses on one's breathing in and out of the nostrils. If one becomes distracted from the breath, one passively notices that one's mind has wandered, but in an accepting, non-judgmental way and one returns to focusing on one's breathing. As one practises meditation regularly, it becomes easier to keep focused on breathing. Awareness of breathing is eventually extended into awareness of thoughts, feelings and actions. This is helpful in making your escape from your nicotine prison.

Your mind and your brain

The mind is a psychological system that is organised in the brain. It is quite complicated but the details do not matter. It helps to understand how the brain controls the mind by discussing the structure of the brain. Essentially, we all have 'three brains in one'. The brain is divided into several parts that have different names. What is important here is to know that three brain systems are necessary for any change to happen. These systems evolved at different stages of evolution: reptilian, mammalian and human. Human brains contain all three systems.

Three Brains in One

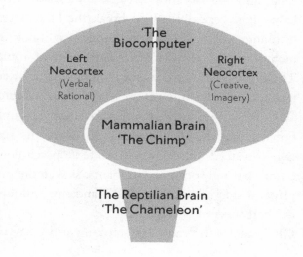

I give the three systems special names to represent the kinds of activities that they perform. They are imaginary characters that illustrate the experiences of smoking and the role of different part of the brain. These are the 'Biocomputer', the 'Chimp' and the 'Chameleon'.

CBT provides a tool set for changing what goes on in the mind, i.e. mental contents, in controlling smoking. The approach of *Stop Smoking Now* is a total one. The objective is to change the mental and physical processes of addiction in their entirety. To achieve this, CBT will be targeted at these three brain functions. Only by making changes throughout the entire system, will you be able to stop smoking now.

Conclusions

1. One reason it is so difficult to stop smoking is that each smoking occasion creates a separate smoking habit. It is very difficult to break the links between smoking and its long-term triggers without using techniques that remove the reward value of smoking.

2. The UK's NHS uses a medical model that is oriented purely towards minimising withdrawal symptoms. Withdrawal is an important part of stopping smoking but it is not the total process. To overcome smoking, you need strategies that tackle its psychological, emotional and social determinants, as well the purely physical side of smoking. CBT and mindfulness are the best ways of doing this.

3. CBT tackles the causes of smoking and puts you in

charge of your own behaviour. CBT explores, and provides ways to change, the thoughts and feelings and actions that make a smoker continue with the habit. It tackles the behaviour itself – when, where and why it happens – and confronts the emotional aspects of smoking.

4. There are three parts of your brain involved in smoking that we call the 'Biocomputer', the 'Chimp' and the 'Chameleon'. It will be necessary to manage all three of these 'brains' and to program them as a team. You will take charge as manager in control of your brain team.

5. You will learn to manage your behaviour, thoughts and feelings. With CBT, you will be in charge of stopping smoking. Follow the strategies offered in this book and you will *Stop Smoking Now* and do it permanently.

PART TWO

STOP SMOKING NOW: THE PROCESS

Part Two guides you through the process that enables you to reduce your smoking to zero. The main features of your mind and brain that you need in order to stop smoking now are your Biocomputer, your inner Chimp and your inner Chameleon. When you have mastered these, you will have mastered your addiction to nicotine.

Chapters 4 to 8 each cover one day of the process. Chapter 4 deals with Day Four and the weekend days leading up to your chosen Stop-Day. Chapter 8 describes in detail exactly how you will deal with your Stop-Day. There's no need to worry, you will get there, and you will be fine.

Each chapter offers skills and strategies that will help you to reduce your consumption and then to stop smoking finally – once and for all. We indicate over the page when the various methods are necessary. Use this schedule as a guide to your journey towards stopping smoking. It's a checklist of when you use the different procedures. Check off the methods that you use each day right up to your 'D-Day' or Stop-Day.

When you reach Part Three, check off the procedures that you introduce at that stage also. By the time you have completed the entire *Stop Smoking Now* process, each of the plus signs should have a tick beside it. Taking Day One as an example: by the end of your first twenty-four-hour period, you should have started to use, and checked under Tuesday's column, methods one to three. By the end of the second twenty-four-hour period on Wednesday, you should have used, and checked under Wednesday's column, methods one to six.

It's that simple, use and tick, use and tick, all the way to the end.

Make Day One a Tuesday. The whole system depends on that. There are many very good reasons why Tuesday should be Day One. Thousands of other smokers have started the process on Tuesday and successfully quit. It's all about successful management of your change and Tuesday has always been the best day to start *Stop Smoking Now*. The next five days, Days Two to Six, are then all fixed in a schedule. Your D-Day or Stop-Day will be a day carefully chosen by you, between Day Seven to Day Ten. Your Stop-Day therefore should be a Monday (Day Seven), a Tuesday (Day Eight), a Wednesday (Day Nine) or a Thursday (Day Ten) in the week following your starting date. Which day you make your Stop-Day is completely your own choice. Choose whichever day you think will give you your best chance of stopping smoking for good.

Please try all of the methods. By doing so, you will give yourself the best possible chance of success.

	Method
1	Rubber Band around Pack
2	Record all Smoking on Card
3	Program 1 **(NURD)**
4	Enter Daily Total on Chart
5	Program 2 **(WE STD)**
6	Keep a List of Triggers
7	Program 3 **(EASY)**
8	Meditation
9	Imagery Rehearsal
10	Program 4 **(NOGO)**
11	The Eight Steps and Sensitization
12	Music Therapy (Side 2, Cassette)
13	Win the Argument Game
14	List Personal Benefits of Quitting
15	Plan Your D-Day
16	Try Different Ways of Relaxing
17	Rehearse Positive Programs
18	Increase Activity
19	Distraction
20	Buddy System
21	Willpower
22	Learn Fail-Safe Procedure
23	Develop Eating Control Programme
24	Rules for Snacking
25	Develop Exercise Programme
26	Relapse Prevention
27	Assert Non-Smokers' Rights
28	Deconstruct Tobacco Advertising
29	Develop Time Management Skills
30	Prevent Stress and Strain

	Tues	Wed	Thurs	Fri	Week-end	D-Day	Post D-Day
1	+	+	+	+	+		
2	+	+	+	+	+		
3	+	+	+	+	+		
4	+	+	+	+	+	+	
5		+	+	+	+	+	
6		+	+	+	+	+	
7			+	+	+	+	
8			+	+	+	+	+
9			+	+	+	+	+
10			+	+	+	+	+
11				+	+	+	+
12				+	+	+	+
13				+	+	+	+
14				+	+		+
15				+	+		
16				+	+	+	+
17					+	+	+
18					+	+	+
19					+	+	+
20					+	+	+
21						+	+
22						+	+
23							+
24							+
25							+
26							+
27							+
28							+
29							+
30							+

4

Day One: Tuesday – deprogramming your mind

Advances in the psychology of behavioural change have led to powerful psychological therapies that enable people to change their habits and addictions without the need for drugs. Cognitive psychologists, who specialise in the investigation of mental processes, focus on human memory, imagery, language, and consciousness. Behavioural psychologists have studied learning, conditioning, addiction and habit-formation. Health psychologists have brought these two strands together to produce effective behaviour change techniques. Cognitive behavioural therapy (CBT) is a special application of this knowledge to emotional problems, habits and addictions. In the remainder of this book, I will take the most advanced theories and discoveries from the science of psychology and apply them to the issue at hand: to stop smoking now.

How your mind works

The mind is organised by different parts of your brain. In *Stop Smoking Now*, three brain parts will be shown to be important. These parts are the three principal 'characters' that play a role in taking back your freedom from addiction. The CBT that you use will be directed at these three characters. You are their director/manager. Like any successful manager or director, you need to coax the three characters to do what you want them to do. The three characters are the 'Biocomputer', the 'Chimp' and the 'Chameleon'. I'll introduce them one by one.

The Biocomputer

The Biocomputer is at the smart end of your brain. It is the most intelligent part. It is logical and rational; it accumulates information in its memory banks, learns, solves problems, gets you from A to B and back again and uses rules and reasoning.

The Biocomputer is your **neocortex**, which consists of two large hemispheres that enable language and abstract thought (on the left side, usually) with imagination and creativity (on the right side, usually). The neocortex is very large (with ten to fourteen billion cells) and it is the fount of human culture. Your identity as a person is based here.

The Biocomputer/neocortex develops as we mature from a child into an adult. It learns through its experiences, its 'programming'. It does not have wants or wishes or desires.

The Biocomputer.

It knows what is good and bad, healthy and unhealthy and what is morally right and wrong. It plans, models and imagines. It is the part of the brain that has decided that you need to stop smoking.

The Biocomputer does what it is programmed to do. Nothing more, nothing less. However, it is very, very smart. It is filled with useful knowledge but it also contains a lot of 'junk mail' that it has collected while you have been watching TV, reading comics or magazines or looking at advertisements. It contains information that is erroneous and wrong, some of which is hazardous to your health.

The Biocomputer tries to control the two other brains, the Chimp and the Chameleon brains. However, this regulation is never a hundred per cent successful. Both of the other brains have independence and can often be 'naughty' and cause you problems – one being your addiction to nicotine.

The Chimp.

The Chimp brain

The Chimp is the emotional brain that feels pleasure and pain, love and caring, fear and depression. Like the Biocomputer, the Chimp is neither all good nor all bad but can be either. The emotional brain records memories of behaviours that produced agreeable and disagreeable experiences. The main structures are the hippocampus, the amygdala and the hypothalamus. The Chimp brain is naturally curious.

It explores new things and learns through the sometimes painful experience of trial and error. Based on its conditioning, the Chimp jumps to opinions very quickly, thinks in black and white, gets paranoid and is irrational. The Chimp brain includes the reward system responsible for producing pleasure that helps to create addictions to drugs such as nicotine. The Chimp is mischievous and generally will find a way to satisfy its desires – if your Biocomputer allows it. The Chimp communicates using drives, feelings and emotions. It does not speak or understand language but does comprehend the tone of a human voice or the look on a person's face. It reads and displays body language.

The Chimp thinks of the Chameleon as its pet. It rewards the Chameleon whenever the Chameleon signals, on autopilot, it needs to eat, drink, nap, or smoke a cigarette.

The Chameleon.

The Chameleon brain

The Chameleon is instinctive and primitive. It reacts to base instincts: wake or sleep, sweat or shiver and fight, flight or freeze. What the Chameleon does is unconscious. It controls the body's vital functions, heart-rate, breathing, body temperature and balance. The Chameleon is the auto-pilot, changing the whole system's state of arousal. You couldn't exist without it. If it goes to sleep, you go to sleep, so it needs to remain alert and to thrive. The Chameleon's small but crucial share of the brain contains the main structures found in any reptilian brain: the brainstem and the cerebellum. The Chameleon brain is 100 per cent reliable but, as a consequence, can be obsessive and compulsive at times. It has its own way of doing things and likes to keep it that way. It can make you feel tired and want to sleep at the wink of an eye. The Chameleon watches over the rest of the system which is its territory, enjoys being in command of your basic bodily functions and carries out other typical 'reptile' behaviours. It needs to be kept interested and well-rewarded or it will simply shut down the entire system like a disgruntled French trade union.

A real-life chameleon is a role model for an addicted smoker. Except it's addicted to crickets. It eats fifteen to fifty crickets a day. That's not smoking cigarettes, but the mechanism is the same. The behaviour is on auto-pilot. The behaviour is immediately rewarded and so it's repeated. As noted, the Chimp likes to think that it has control over the Chameleon. However, deep-down it's the Chameleon that is in control of the Chimp and also the Biocomputer. It can arouse the whole system, wake it up or send it to sleep, make it break into a sweat, get it into dangerous places by making it fight instead of flee. Just for fun, let's call the

Chameleon by the nickname of 'Zee' (as in the American way of saying the last letter of the alphabet).

Your brain parts must work as a team

One of the main problems of your addiction is that the different parts of your brain are at loggerheads. Quite often they are not pulling in the same direction. They are not working together as a team. There is a wise saying, often attributed to Aristotle: 'The whole is greater than the sum of the parts'. This is certainly the case when it comes to smoking. You need to get the whole system to pull together. You simply can't win otherwise. You need to get to know the team members, understand 'what makes them tick'.

It may seem shocking at first to suggest that the human brain has part-brains inside it. But we all have them. There's no shame in having three part-brains that affect what we do and how we feel but, if you think about it, it's not actually that strange at all. Human beings evolved after hundreds of millions years and, although we like to consider ourselves as being at the high point of the evolutionary tree, there is little to back up that assertion. Yes, we may have sent rockets into space and walked on the moon, but we're not doing very well when it comes to looking after ourselves or the planet that we live on.

The Biocomputer is perhaps the pride and joy of the evolutionary tree, but the tree's trunk lies rooted in the prehistoric past. It is our hedonistic, pleasure-seeking drive that push us to do some of our most stupid things. These, needless to say, include smoking. Our most caring side is coming from the Chimp inside. It is nurturing and wants to be loved and to give love. Part of that involves caring, eating, drinking and, unfortunately – now you are addicted – smoking. Our most basic functions are controlled by the Chameleon, our alertness, arousal, and momentum. All three brains together make up your brain team.

It hardly needs saying that the three brains, the Biocomputer, the Chimp and Zee, are not always good team players. They have different priorities and objectives, different skills and different values. This can lead to anarchy. Especially when there is a lack of strong leadership. We need to pull these parts together so that they work as a team. You need to regain your control as manager and coach of your team. That's what *Stop Smoking Now* is here for. *Stop Smoking Now* could really be titled *Start Managing Now*. Start managing your brain team to play together, stop the conflict and competition that exists between the different brain-parts. If the Chameleon runs off in one direction and does its own thing, the Chimp goes off somewhere else, and the Biocomputer sits waiting for instructions and is confused then we have no chance of winning the change game. The change game is the only game in town. Stand still as a smoker and you're dead. You really must take charge and manage the three players.

To get the team to play well together, you need to be an effective coach of the three players. Unless you get your three part-brains to learn to play properly together, you cannot make the changes that you want in your life. You will remain enslaved by old habits controlled by the Chimp and Zee. To stop smoking now, you need to manage your mind. Failure is not an option.

Here is your team diagram:

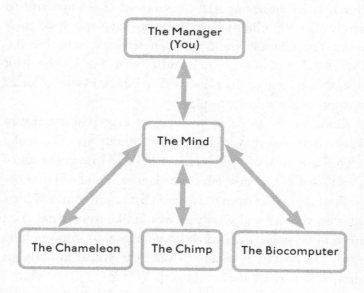

The brain team.

In managing the team you have many wonderful resources. The mind is one of your most valuable assets. Another highly valuable asset is your physical body. If you are a believer, your spiritual being is a third asset. In addition, please do not forget that you have your support team: your family, friends and work colleagues who are there to help and support you while you are making this wonderful change. You need all of your resources. Try your best to get everybody on board. 'A friend in need, is a friend indeed.'

Within your mind, the Biocomputer is the most intelligent and flexible asset. However, intelligence is not everything. Even more important is wisdom. It is important to know that the Chimp and Zee also have minds of their own. The Chimp's mind makes it sensitive, intuitive and lovable. Zee is sweet, quick and protean but can be a bit distant and strange. Its mind is tiny but can cause a lot of disruption if it decides to play up.

Consider the fact that you cannot exist without any of your assets and they cannot exist without you. To make a profound change, you need to be able to manage all of these assets in the most effective manner. You need to show leadership, to lead from the front. That requires mindfulness of who you are and who you would like to become. You need to be single-minded about your goal to stop smoking now. Do not listen to any of the little voices inside your mind that may try to distract you.

One reason you sometimes feel confused as a smoker is that you have up to three different 'voices' telling you things. Although the Chimp cannot actually talk, it can send you moods and feelings, urges to smoke and cravings when you haven't smoked for a while. Zee can make you drowsy because it's running down your body clock towards sleep-time or arouse you and keep you awake when you want to sleep. It can be a proper little nuisance at times. The Biocomputer pays attention to your schedule and sends you thoughts such as, 'Get yourself ready for tomorrow's meeting with the boss'. 'Prepare that progress report'. This is what it means when a person speaks of being in two minds about something. Very often there is a conflict between their instructions: 'Go and have that chocolate bar and a nice smoke,' might come from the Chimp mind, with vital functions – 'Go have a pee' – coming via the Chameleon mind and the rational mind, 'Go finish that report,' says the Biocomputer. The first two want to make you feel good, while the third wants you to be sensible, organised and get things done. Something has to give.

Almost certainly, under all these circumstances, as a smoker, you will have a smoke, and maybe eat the chocolate bar as well. What else can you do? You will see a better option later in this book (see page 201).

To make it possible to stop smoking now, in your role as manager, you need to work with the Biocomputer, the Chimp and the Chameleon to ensure that they are all pulling in the same direction as you. You need harmony in the system. There's no point in being in two minds or even in three minds about stopping smoking now. Without the help of the Biocomputer, the Chimp and Zee, you will definitely struggle. Fortunately, the techniques that you will learn offer excellent methods for reprogramming your Biocomputer. Once that has happened, Chimp and Zee will fall into line. But they will need some special coaxing because, until now, they have been running the show.

Your brain, thought, emotion and behaviour are all interconnected in the Brain Pyramid (see illustration below).

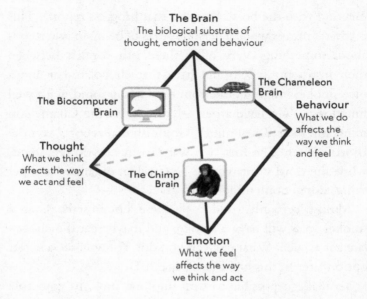

The brain pyramid.

The role of the Biocomputer

The Biocomputer brain is your information processor and main memory bank. Logical, rational and highly competent, it is spread through different regions of the brain. It is the hardware. With the help of the Chameleon's awareness and arousal functions, Chimp's urges and cravings and your Biocomputer's love of order, you have acquired many programs that are stored in your Biocomputer mind. These programs are the 'software' of your mind. The programs dictate what you do, when you do it and how you do it. These follow years of learning and experience, much of which came about due to the natural curiosity of the Chimp. And, of course, the routines of the auto-pilot Chameleon. Other things you learned from your parents, teachers at school, from your friends and through newspapers, magazines, tablets and smart phones or by watching television.

When we learn new skills, we need to go slowly at first, until the processes become automatic. Think of how you learned to ride a bicycle. There's a lot of mental activity going on beneath the surface of conscious awareness. Our thoughts, feelings, and behaviour are quite often controlled by unconscious mental processes. A lot of what we do – including some quite complicated activities, such as speaking, shuffling a pack of playing cards and riding a bicycle – is controlled automatically by hidden mental processes that are exactly like computer programs. These automatic activities are the results of long periods of learning and all habits and skills are learned behaviours.

Once these skills and habits are established, the Chameleon takes over. It is perfectly suited to the repetition of skilful, well-learned tasks. When a chameleon sees a cricket, its sticky tongue comes right out and it gobbles it up. A real chameleon's tongue projection is fast, reaching the prey in as little as 0.07 seconds. Your Chameleon brain is slower than that in reaching for a cigarette, but it's quite rapid and it's carried out on auto-pilot without any conscious thinking. That's how the Chameleon always operates, on auto-pilot, changing your state of arousal and awareness and making automatic responses.

Loss of conscious control over routine action has some obvious advantages. Imagine how difficult and tedious life would be if we had to consciously plan every word we spoke or every movement we made in performing everyday tasks. There would simply be too much to think about, and our ability to co-ordinate our thoughts and actions would quickly break down.

When you smoke, you are operating on automatic pilot. You are not consciously in control of what you are doing. At times, the automatic programming of your behaviour is not entirely to your liking and you would prefer to behave differently, if you were only able to do so. But your auto-pilot Chameleon does not relinquish control when you want it to and so you are left repeating unwanted behaviour with little conscious ability to do anything to stop it from happening. All of your automatic behaviour is controlled by the Chameleon. Much of the repetitious and ritualistic action that the Chameleon performs is useful, but some of it is a nuisance. The Chameleon is a sticker, a persistent little beast that never gives up. Until you make it stop, that is. You need to manage it better and you can, helped by CBT.

But having a Chameleon on auto-pilot does not mean that our conduct is necessarily entirely out of our voluntary control. It is possible to use the rest of our brain power to control our automatic actions. That is what we are doing here in *Stop Smoking Now*. We are learning to manage automatic responses using the Biocomputer. Even the most ingrained habits can be brought under voluntary control by systematically breaking them down into their components and making these components more deliberate and voluntary. Eventually, a whole habit or routine can be returned to its original non-automatic state, through a process of relearning or what is really re-programming. The objective of CBT is to eliminate the automatic nature of smoking by deliberately influencing the thoughts and feelings that occur before, during and after smoking. We take back control by reprogramming our Biocomputer.

The Biocomputer is an extremely complicated device, but having fine hardware is not sufficient in itself to guarantee a sensible result. The human Biocomputer needs orderly programming if it is to function usefully.

As we mature and our minds develop, we acquire ways of thinking, behaving, and feeling. We acquire these ways of being through observing and interacting with others and by reacting to events that happen, many of them completely beyond our control. Much of our early behaviour involves learning by trial and error, with associated rewards and punishments. This is the process psychologists call 'conditioning'. The Chimp is the primary actor in this process but Zee's role is also vital because it's this little critter at the base of our brain that keeps us alert and focused.

Later, after extensive trial and error learning through the natural curiosity of the Chimp, our thinking, habits, and emotional reactions become relatively fixed and we operate more predictably – like a computer that has been programmed to process information in particular ways.

Unfortunately, not all of our programming is sensible and rational and we may end up doing some unhealthy things, such as smoking. Our brains are responsible for everything we think, feel, and do. In the case of a smoker, the entire brain team is programmed by the addiction process to carry out smoking, in the same way that a computer is programmed to carry out automatic functions.

When we describe smoking as a 'habit' or 'addiction', we are referring to its automatic, compulsive nature and the way in which a smoker no longer feels any real sense of control over when, where and how much to smoke. It is therefore quite legitimate to think of the smoking habit as an automatic function of a biocomputer that is programmed to smoke.

The same programming is responsible for generating the desire to smoke when no nicotine has entered the body for an hour or two. The programming generates enjoyable feelings during smoking, especially when the desire to smoke has built up to be quite strong. CBT to the rescue! Using CBT you will be able to eliminate all of your automatic programs. This will involve all three members of your brain team.

Eliminating automatic programs

Let's look at a typical smoker aged around thirty who took up smoking at fourteen and smokes an average of just under twenty-five cigarettes per day. This means that they have smoked a total of 90,400 cigarettes since starting the habit. Assuming an average puff rate of eleven puffs per cigarette and an average of 346 seconds to smoke a cigarette, the typical young smoker will have taken nearly one million puffs and spent the equivalent of 362 days – or just under one year – smoking! Makes you think doesn't it? You may wish to calculate your own figures, if you'd like a bit more of an incentive to quit.

So a regular smoker aged only thirty has spent a whole year of their life smoking. This figure would be even higher for older smokers or those who smoke more than twenty-five cigarettes per day. The twenty-five-a-day smoker is effectively spending 36.5 days each year smoking – that is, more than one month. And in that time the smoker will have taken a hundred thousand puffs!

A very sizeable percentage of this smoking activity is carried out without the smoker even thinking about what is going on. Because of its automatic nature, the behaviour has been programmed and controlled by the Chameleon under the instructions of the Biocomputer. This programming is acquired during the first few experiences of smoking, which typically occur between the ages of ten and fifteen years. So where does the smoking habit come from?

The Biocomputer tells us that it's unhealthy and bad, that it stinks, and makes us smelly, but we can't stop doing it. What the heck is going on? It's a simple case of the different brains with different priorities seeking overall control. We've already discussed the mischievous role of the Chameleon. But in the mischievous stakes, the Chameleon has nothing compared to the Chimp. The Chimp is top of the tree when it comes to plain naughtiness.

It is the Chimp's constant search for satisfaction and its desperate seeking of approval, that are the main drivers of habit formation. The Chimp is continuously searching for a reward, something to eat, something to drink, something novel to do, some variety, some spice and some attention. It is the restless part of our mind that is never quite satisfied. The Chimp is the one that says, 'More, more, more!' when we're already full, already tipsy, or having plenty of fun. The Chimp is in control of our emotions and gets down, gets stressed, craves and cries and has a need for comfort and satisfaction. As we acquire the habit of smoking, it is the cheeky Chimp and the Chimp alone, who drives us on the path to more and more consumption. It is the Chimp who ensures that the Biocomputer's logic and rationality is dumbfounded by the sheer greedy naughtiness of having more than we need of any good thing. It's the Chimp who makes too much of a good thing and has the ability to turn it sour. The Chimp is like a child, never knowing when to stop. Then it often ends in tears. The Chimp is often a chump, but a lovable chump.

Programs are acquired through many different routes: watching TV or movies, using apps, playing games and imitation, peer pressure, advertising. The addictive effects of nicotine makes the smoker want to continue. Remember this – the Chimp loves to imitate. It loves to conform. It is needy. It is greedy. It's easily bored. It's restless. It fidgets a lot. It's childish. These are some of the main reasons you took up smoking in the first place. It was your Chimp and its little friend, Zee, who got you into the habit. The Biocomputer simply absorbed all of the new programming that came along with the new activity of smoking. It had little choice. It can only accept, not reject programs. These Chimp and Zee factors contribute to the mental programs that keep you smoking. The trouble is that, although the Biocomputer knows perfectly well that the smoking programs are very bad programs and should be got rid of, it didn't put them there in the first place and can't get rid of them without the help and cooperation of the Chimp and the Chameleon.

Basically, you, the manager, lost the plot. The different brains all started their different games and you let them run rampant. Your team went walkabout and your mind went AWOL. You ceased to be a manager.

Once smoking became routine, you allowed Chimp and Zee basically to run things their way and, shirked responsibility. At this point, your addiction to nicotine was complete.

The Chameleon and the Chimp don't really care. Both are happy for you to continue smoking. They hate change.

They are both doing their job of finding satisfaction and repeating a simple skill. The act of smoking is reinforced by Chimp's satisfaction, which is provided by each new shot of nicotine, courtesy of Chameleon's auto-pilot actions. No real thinking or control is actually required. It's only if you take your role as manager more seriously that you can use the Biocomputer's superior intelligence to stop smoking now.

You need to take back the control of your mind. You do this by reprogramming the Biocomputer. The things you need to do in order to stop smoking are:

- Take back control from Chimp who keeps the programs running because it gets satisfaction.
- Take back control from Chameleon who loves the power of pleasing the Chimp for rewards.

Taking back control from the Chimp and the Chameleon is a matter of some importance and urgency. CBT helps you to achieve this efficiently and permanently by working on the hidden mechanisms which make you think, feel, and behave as a smoker.

If you follow the procedures carefully, you will eliminate all desire to smoke. After a few days, cigarettes will give you no satisfaction and smoking them will feel unpleasant.

Motivation

The strength of your motivation is a key factor in successfully overcoming your smoking habit. Think about why you want to give up smoking. Is it because you're worried about your health? Or because the habit is becoming a drain on your finances? Write these reasons down and keep them somewhere handy so you can look at them when you feel like giving up your efforts to quit smoking.

Self-belief

Many of us are limited by our own ideas about what we think we can achieve. This is frequently much less than our true potential. One of the biggest difficulties faced by smokers is the conviction that failure is inevitable.

If you are confident that you will achieve your goal, you will be in a better position to do so. Any lurking self-doubts need to be eliminated right now. If you believe that your chances of stopping smoking are only slight, you will sabotage even the most carefully designed program. Tell yourself that, in seven to ten days, you will be a non-smoker and enjoy life much more than you do now. Become optimistic. Become enthusiastic. Most of all, become confident in your own ability to overcome smoking.

To encourage yourself to think more positively, examine the progress chart printed in Appendix A. Photocopy it and keep it where you can see it throughout the day. Look at it often: in the mornings when you get up, and last thing at night before you go to bed. Remember that, when you look at this chart, you are seeing the same goals thousands of smokers have already achieved before you. There is absolutely no reason why your progress should be any different!

How CBT can work for you

You are starting a tried and tested psychological approach that identifies and removes the triggers for smoking that are unique to you as a smoker. If you continue to follow the process, you definitely will stop smoking now.

How can I state this with such confidence? Firstly, research with thousands of smokers has shown that CBT records a success rate that is much higher than trying to stop smoking on your own. CBT has been thoroughly evaluated before being released and the results have been independently verified and published in scientific reports. The system has been proven to work, as long as you stick to it.

Secondly, I strongly encourage you to use this carefully chosen set of procedures, enabling you to tap mental powers and abilities which function very efficiently when you are undergoing a major lifestyle change. You may be amazed at how successful these procedures can be, once you start to apply them systematically.

Thirdly, the system is effective because it helps you to uncover the immediate triggers of your smoking and to eliminate your desire to smoke and the associated enjoyment and the satisfaction. Any method failing to address these motivating factors will fail to bring about a successful outcome.

Fourthly, the need to use willpower is kept to the absolute minimum: it is unnecessary to fight a mental battle or make enormous efforts to change your behaviour. When you are trying to use willpower, you are fighting with your inner

Chimp and Zee. Normally, they will win. They never want to change. They like things as they are. But you do not need to feel any great stress or strain because you will not have to go to extreme lengths to stop smoking. Changing behaviour – learning new skills and unlearning old ones – can be done in a relaxed and natural way. The Biocomputer and the other members of your brain team will change their response to stimuli when the usual rewards are no longer present.

To obtain the best results, please try to keep your mind as open as possible to the ideas in CBT. Free yourself from the worry that you have been unable to stop smoking in the past. The more you try to enjoy the process of participating in this CBT process, the easier it should be to obtain the desired result. So try to have fun while you prove to yourself that you can stop smoking now.

Noticing your automatic smoking chains

Every time you have a cigarette, an automatic chain of smoking responses is activated. In its most extreme form, this automatic chain can be carried out without a single conscious thought about what is happening.

A typical automatic chain consists of the following links:

1. Trigger stimulus.
2. Reach for packet.
3. Hold packet in one hand.
4. Remove one cigarette.

5.   Place cigarette in mouth.
6.   Find lighter or matches.
7.   Light cigarette.
8.   Inhale first puff.
9.   Exhale first puff.
10. Place cigarette in ash tray.
11. Pick up cigarette from ash tray.
12. Inhale second puff.
13. Exhale second puff.
14–30. Another nine or so puffs.
31. Put down cigarette.
32. Stub cigarette out.

This automatic chain, or a variation of it, is repeated every time a smoker has a cigarette. It is carried out by Zee, the Chameleon, without even thinking.

It does it the same way each and every time. Because the chain is very difficult to stop once it has been started, you need to use a method to alert yourself when the chain is about to start. A simple technique has been designed specifically for this purpose.

To help you notice each time you take a cigarette from the packet, place a rubber band around your packet. You will have to remove this before you take out each new cigarette. When you have finished taking out a cigarette (and completed the reduction card procedure described in the next section) make sure that your rubber band goes back onto your packet. The rubber band is a form of mindfulness. You make an activity that is carried out unconsciously – or 'mindlessly' – into a conscious action again. The rubber band is a protective device that gives you an alarm signal every time you have a cigarette, to warn you that your automatic smoking chain is being 'pulled' yet again. It therefore provides the first important step in successfully breaking the habit of smoking. By stopping the chain at the very beginning, you will eventually be able to gain control of the situation. The rubber band also allows you to think about the trigger stimulus that is making you want to have a cigarette at the particular moment that you are removing it from the packet.

Using your Daily Reduction Cards

It is important that you make a record of every cigarette you smoke from the date you start the CBT process until you have completely stopped, so please carry a pen or pencil with you at all times. Photocopy Appendix B, where you will find a set of Daily Reduction Cards for you to cut out of the photocopied sheet and insert into your cigarette pack. When you decide to have a cigarette, put a little '1' by the hour of day marked on the card. You will soon see what sort of smoking pattern emerges. Perhaps for you there are certain times of the day when you smoke more. These periods may be associated with tension or other moods or feelings.

Start a new card each day that you are in this process and every night enter the total number of cigarettes you have smoked on your progress chart. You will be able to see the drop-off in cigarette consumption with every day you use the *Stop Smoking Now* process. Nine cards are provided, which will last until your Stop-Day (no later than Day Ten). The progress chart shows a set of daily targets that you should aim to reach, starting with your current daily level as 100 per cent. These reduce by 40 to 50 per cent each day, allowing your smoking to gradually taper off.

If your current level is twenty cigarettes per day then you should aim to reduce this to twelve to fifteen cigarettes on Day One, seven to nine cigarettes on Day two, three to four cigarettes on Day Three, two to three cigarettes on Day Four, one to two cigarettes on Day five, and then zero or one cigarette on Day Six. Your Stop-Day could be Day Seven, Eight, Nine or, at the latest, Day Ten, when you definitely should not smoke. You choose your Stop-Day, ideally two days beforehand, so you have a concrete target in mind. I describe the procedures for establishing the exact date for your Stop-Day in Chapter 8.

How to deprogram your mind

At the moment, your mind contains the mental programming of a smoker. This is because your Biocomputer automatically plays the programs that give you the desire to smoke when it is presented with certain kinds of stimulation. When you see, hear, smell or feel a trigger – or if you have not smoked for a certain period of time, and the nicotine level in your body is running low – a message is automatically sent to the Biocomputer, asking you to top up your nicotine levels. The Biocomputer responds and begins to correct the situation. In order to top up the amount of nicotine in the body, you must be made to want to smoke a cigarette. The Biocomputer sends a craving feeling to your conscious mind and you then experience a conscious desire for a cigarette. Quite automatically, you pick up a cigarette and smoke it to satisfy your craving and the brain team gives you a conscious feeling of pleasure or satisfaction in its place. This cycle of events is repeated over and over again.

The cycle looks like this:

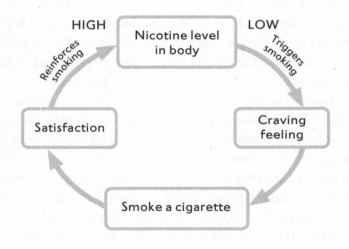

Our smoking is strongly rewarded. Notice also that the sequence switches from conscious experience to unconscious programming quite automatically. This makes it very difficult to intervene and interrupt the cycle.

It is important to remember that your Biocomputer did not always operate in this way. Once upon a time you would never have craved a cigarette. It should not be long before you return to that state. All you need to do is to change your current programming in your Biocomputer. In effect, your mind and body will revert back to their original state before you took up smoking. All the learning that took place during your initiation to smoking – and after your habit was established – will be completely reversed. For example, once upon a time you enjoyed a meal or a drink without needing to have a smoke. Perhaps these days you always smoke after your dinner and while having a cup of tea or coffee. The signal comes – 'dinner over, coffee made' – and the Biocomputer automatically responds by playing the 'I want a cigarette now' program. You respond automatically and, if possible, light up. If you need to go outside to do so, you excuse yourself and leave.

Because of the multiple repetitions of the pairing of coffee with smoking, you now respond automatically to programmed instructions to smoke and this makes you feel as though you have very little choice. If you decide not to have a cigarette, you become involved in an extremely difficult battle. You are forced to use your willpower, to fight against the Chimp to resist the temptation of having a cigarette. If you rely on your inner Chimp to cease wanting satisfaction from smoking, you are likely to lose, and you may have to suffer the consequences of withdrawal. The sequence then looks like this:

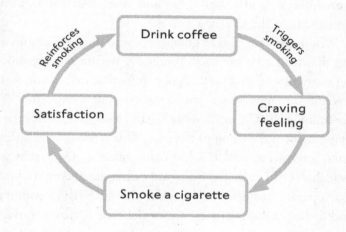

In this case, by not smoking you are punishing the Chimp and it will get up to all sorts of tricks until you are likely to give into your craving when it becomes too strong to resist. Once again, the sequence of events switches from conscious to unconscious, which means that you have great difficulty controlling it. While you may feel pleased with yourself at an intellectual level for resisting the drive to smoke, your act of consciously resisting smoking is not being rewarded at a feeling level. It is the feeling level that dominates the experience of the addict. This is your Chimp level. This is why willpower is not enough. You are placing your Chimp in conflict with your Biocomputer. CBT will enable you to remove the conflict by changing your experience of smoking from a pleasant to an unpleasant experience and eliminating your desire to smoke altogether. The Chimp won't like it, and it will rebel and resist, but the CBT is stronger than the Chimp.

When we talk about giving up smoking, or eliminating the drug nicotine from the body, we are talking about deprogramming that part of your mind that makes you restless and unhappy when you deny yourself a cigarette. We are training the Chimp and the Chameleon that smoking is a dying habit and a thing of the past. This is the radical difference between using CBT and many other methods that are available. CBT uses psychological principles and procedures that operate simultaneously at the thinking (Biocomputer) and feeling (Chimp) levels. Once the feeling that you want to smoke is gone, the Chimp will stop fretting and the immediate cause of your smoking will have been removed. You will then be completely free of the habit. Your inner trio will all get on with other things. Chimp and Zee have very short memories and they won't bear a grudge. The Biocomputer has no feelings. It's basically a robot. It does what it's programmed to do, nothing more, nothing less.

It is entirely up to you how thoroughly you are prepared to work at deprogramming your desire to smoke and thus not have to cope with that awful craving feeling. Some people completely deprogram themselves in a matter of days and their desire to smoke is reduced to zero. Others deprogram themselves sufficiently well to make the fight against their smoking desire an easier one to handle.

Nobody who uses these methods consistently and patiently should fail to destroy all of their enjoyment of smoking. If that enjoyment is not destroyed, you will carry on doing it. The inner Chimp, Chameleon and Biocomputer are waiting for you to give your instructions to stop smoking now!

Waiting for your instructions to stop smoking now.

Program 1

When you draw on a cigarette, hot, poisonous fumes enter your respiratory system and burn your throat, irritate and destroy the delicate tissues in your lungs, and eventually cause a 'smoker's cough'. How is it possible that you can feel pleasure, enjoyment, and satisfaction?

The answer, of course, is that part of your brain naturally gives you a feeling of pleasure when nicotine enters your body and dopamine is released in the pleasure centres of the Chimp brain. At the same time, your body has adapted to the naturally unpleasant sensations of the smoke and is now fully capable of screening most of them out.

Consider what happens to non-smokers, when for some reason they decide to smoke a cigarette. With the first puff the heart begins to beat more rapidly, mainly due to the effect of the drug nicotine. The amount of oxygen absorbed into the bloodstream decreases because the poisonous gas carbon monoxide is absorbed instead. With a lowered supply of oxygen to the brain, the person will probably begin to feel dizzy and their head will start to ache. They may feel quite ill and experience nausea. If they try to smoke more than one cigarette, they may even vomit.

How does a smoker's programming become so powerful? There are many different ways. Among the most important are social pressure, cigarette advertising and social conditioning. Rebelling against authority figures is also a factor, especially in the ten- to fourteen-year-old age group, when most smokers take up the habit. Once smoking has started, all of these pressures are reinforced by the addictive qualities of the drug nicotine, and Pro-Cigarette Programs (PCPs) become deeply embedded in the Biocomputer mind.

Here is an example of the kind of program that automatically begins to run through your mind when you light a cigarette:

Ah . . . that feels better. I really needed this cigarette.
I'm enjoying this cigarette. It satisfies me. It relaxes
me. I feel more alive, more stimulated. I am enjoying
myself. That's better. I feel good.

The aim of using CBT is to completely remove this deluding programming so that, when you inhale the poisonous fumes of a cigarette, your Biocomputer does not play you this misleading message. When you draw cigarette smoke into your lungs, you need to be told what is really happening to your body. This can be achieved by deliberately and consciously repeating a more accurate program in your mind during the process of smoking. Your new program must state exactly what messages you want your Biocomputer to produce in the future. At first you will still be under the influence of your old programming and you won't experience all the effects of the new program immediately. But, by repeating the new program with each and every cigarette, your Biocomputer will gradually absorb it and repeat it during the act of smoking. Your Biocomputer, like any computer, will not object to the new program if it is consistent.

A highly effective substitute program is given below. I call it Program 1. Please learn it and repeat it to yourself every time you smoke a cigarette from now on. When you do so regularly you will quickly discover that your cigarette consumption is dropping rather dramatically. Within twenty-four-hours your consumption should be reduced by 25 to 50 per cent. It is necessary to learn it by heart and use it every time you have a cigarette from now on.

The following condensed version may help you to memorise Program 1:

PROGRAM 1

As I smoke I realise that:

This cigarette is giving me no satisfaction.
This is an unpleasant experience.
This cigarette is making me feel rotten.
I am losing the desire to smoke.

NO SATISFACTION	N
UNPLEASANT	U
ROTTEN	R
DESIRE	D

The four key letters N, U, R, D spell a made-up word or mnemonic 'NURD' (similar to the word 'NERD') to help you to remember the whole program.

Notice that NURD operates at the thinking, feeling and behavioural levels at the same time. The Biocomputer, Chimp and Chameleon are all receiving the same message. Chimp and Chameleon don't understand words as such; they only understand the tone and tenor of the communication. The 'ambience' and timing, if you like. Saying and thinking 'NURD' allows all three realise that you are not enjoying smoking anymore and that it is giving you no satisfaction – and this is done while you are in the act of smoking.

The Chameleon and the Chimp are both wonderfully alert to the environment. Normally, when you have a smoke, you and your two inmates just sit back, so to speak, and enjoy it. But when you start 'NURDing', they both can feel that there has been a major intervention in their enjoyment, peace and calm. In other words, the goal to overcome smoking is being realised at all three levels at the same time. The levels are no longer in conflict. This is more consistent than willpower, which always generates conflict.

From now on, you should smoke every cigarette deliberately and with concentration. If you are able to, stop whatever you are doing for a few minutes and really concentrate on your smoking. Repeat the program to yourself. When you say to yourself, 'This is an unpleasant experience,' think about the parts of our body which are directly affected by this unpleasant experience – your tongue, mouth, throat and lungs and feel especially the extra strain being placed upon your heart. At first you may not actually experience anything as being very unpleasant. However, keep repeating the program every time you smoke. Within a day, you will notice that this has dramatically affected the way you experience cigarette smoking.

It is important that you use Program 1 every time you have a cigarette. Recite it automatically to yourself while you are smoking.

Remember to make use of the letters NURD that are printed at the top of the Daily Reduction Cards. Use each letter as you glance at the card in the packet, to remind you of Program 1 while you are smoking:

N = No satisfaction U = Unpleasant R = Rotten D = Desire

Think or say a line of Program 1 to yourself with each new puff of your cigarette. Smoke the cigarette right through and then stub it out. Make sure you've marked your Daily Reduction Card in the correct time slot, put it safely back inside your cigarette packet and replace the rubber band around the packet. Everything is now in place for your next cigarette.

The deeper meaning of Program 1

Program 1 uses mindfulness, increasing awareness of smoking and the effects on the body and the mind. Let's consider the meaning of Program 1 line by line.

Line 1: 'As I smoke I realise that . . . '

This line comes from mindfulness – being in the moment, increasing your awareness of what is happening each and every time that you smoke. Your realization about the effects of smoking will become clearer, more crystallised, more definite each time you say Program 1.

Line 2: 'This cigarette is giving me no satisfaction'

This line is concerned with the fact that you are becoming gradually aware that the search for satisfaction, what you crave as a smoker, is futile. You want satisfaction, but the cigarette that you are smoking now, in the present, is incapable of giving you that precious commodity. It is what you crave most as a human being who is in a constant search to end suffering. In Buddhism, humans suffer because we continually strive after things that do not give lasting happiness. We desperately try to hold on to things – friends, health, material things – that do not last and this causes sorrow. The Buddha pointed out that none of them last and our attachment to them only causes more suffering. The teachings of Buddha were focused entirely on the problem of attachment and its solution. We need to recognise the impermanence of all things and free oneself from attachment to these things. This will greatly lessen our suffering. As a smoker, your realisation that smoking a cigarette does not bring you satisfaction is an important step towards stopping the habit.

Line 3: 'This is an unpleasant experience'

This line is another reference to the fact that *the source of all our daily problems and suffering is our uncontrolled desire, also known as 'attachment'. We want the smoking to give pleasure. But in reality it does not deliver pleasure. It only removes craving. We all have an uncontrolled desire for things that we believe should make us happy. If we were able to control our desire for these things, habits, beliefs, certain people and relationships, there would be no basis to experience the usual problems that occur with such attachments. Uncontrolled desire is the cause of all problems experienced by living beings.* Unless we control our desire our problems will never cease. Anyone who does not wish to experience problems and suffering can learn to control their desire through training in meditation and living in the present with mindfulness.

Line 4: 'This cigarette is making me feel rotten'

This line is another reference to the real experience of smoking, not the experience that you have learned to expect. With your increasing awareness of the true nature of smoking, you are learning that it is only because of your strong desire to smoke, built up by your addiction, that you have any sensation of pleasure. When you analyse it properly you can see that it isn't pleasure at all. It real feeling is quite the opposite; it is a strong sensation of rottenness. Smoking is rotten to its core. It is a dirty, disgusting, despicable habit that is making you feel progressively more and more rotten.

Line 5: 'I am losing the desire to smoke'

This final line of Program 1 summarises the whole purpose of the program. You know that you have an unhealthy desire that you must learn to free yourself from. The fifth line of Program 1 reflects freedom from desire, another key concept from Buddhism. The story about the farmer and the horse in Part One of this book helps to explain the links between thinking and feeling, the fact that nothing is good or bad but thinking makes it so. Desire is based on attachment, something you crave because you believe that it is making your life better and happier. As a smoker that is what you believe and feel about smoking. You desire to smoke because you believe that it is necessary for your happiness. Nothing could be further from the truth. Your supposed desire for cigarettes is a complete fabrication, manufactured from advertisements, the chemical addiction and the belief that you have that you cannot control it. This belief is completely false. You can control it, you can control it right now, you can stop smoking now.

Why Program 1 is more effective than using willpower

We have already illustrated one way in which CBT is superior to willpower. It's a battle between you – the manager using CBT – and your brain team, consisting of the Biocomputer, Chimp and Zee. The feeling, thinking and behavioural levels need to be brought into harmony without nicotine. Here, we look at another aspect of the problem with willpower as a means for changing your behaviour.

It is a basic principle of *Stop Smoking Now* not to use willpower. Why? Let's look at the consequences of using willpower. As a smoker, there are two conflicting parts to your personality. For convenience we shall label these 'Smoker' and 'Non-smoker'. Smoker is the dependent, emotional, more childish part of your character who tends to give in easily to problems and stress and who usually ends up craving a smoke. Basically, it's your Chimp. Non-smoker is the more independent, rational, and mature adult who really does want to stop smoking now and to develop healthier ways of coping with difficulties. This is you – the manager and the long-suffering but not pro-active Biocomputer.

The Biocomputer processes any information that it is given. It rejects nothing. It accepts everything. It's like a library of knowledge, with so much good information, that also includes a large section for comics and magazines that are filled with junk.

Let's look at what happens if you try to use willpower to stop smoking with this kind of 'double personality'. Consider two groups of smokers. The first group are trying to give up by themselves using their willpower. They are relying on their inner Chimps. They haven't smoked for half an hour and are beginning to experience the desire to smoke. The Non-smoker part of them, their managers, decide to put it off and not have a cigarette for a while.

They carry on with some activity but, all the time, the Chimp is getting restless, generating thoughts about smoking and the desire to smoke actually becomes stronger. The Non-smoker manager resists having a cigarette, the Smoker Chimp feels like smoking, and the conscious desire actually becomes stronger. There is now a complete split in personality, and they feel torn between smoking and non-smoking. Finally, there is a complete breakdown and the desire to smoke becomes so strong that the Chimp wins. They light up, and exactly as expected, enjoy it. The desire to smoke will return in another half an hour and the whole cycle of events will be repeated.

What does this do to the programming inside the head? It reinforces smoking very strongly! When feelings of tension are reduced immediately after a cigarette is lit, the act of smoking is strongly rewarded. By using willpower to stop smoking, the desire to smoke becomes stronger and the smoking habit is unlikely to be changed. When the desire to smoke is at its strongest, the smoker is rewarded by the enjoyment of the cigarette. Thus, using willpower makes it more difficult to eliminate smoking because the mental programs which cause the smoking become even more deeply reinforced.

Now let's look at a group of smokers who are using Program 1. When smokers in this group begin to experience the desire to smoke, instead of delaying lighting up and letting the desire get stronger, they tackle the problem while it is still weak. These smokers sit down and, while lighting up, begin to control what they are thinking about. They think and say to themselves the four lines of NURD. They begin to repeat, 'This cigarette is giving me no satisfaction' and they take a deep inhalation from the cigarette, deliberately making themselves aware of the unpleasant effects that the smoke is having. This is relatively easy to do because the desire to smoke is not all that strong. Then, consciously saying to themselves, 'This is an unpleasant experience', the smokers take another deep inhalation. Again, with one deep inhalation each time, the lines, 'This cigarette is making me feel rotten' and 'I am losing the desire to smoke' are repeated.

By this stage, the smoking experience is becoming uncomfortable and unpleasant. The Biocomputer begins to interpret what is happening to the smoker's body more accurately. Smokers using this procedure actually do begin to experience smoking as an unpleasant and sometimes even a painful experience. Smokers in this group finish their cigarettes to the very end, and, realizing that it is extremely uncomfortable to smoke in this manner, deliberately use the cigarette itself to begin the important task of destroying the programs that are responsible for keeping the habit going. Once they've put the cigarette out, it may be several hours before they experience the desire to smoke again. One of the main outcomes of using Program 1 is that it opens up your awareness to what is actually happening when you smoke. It is also a statement of being less satisfied, about freeing yourself from desire. In other words, it is employing a mindfulness of smoking.

There will be variation between individuals but, for each person using Program 1, the time between cigarettes will increase and the desire will decrease until it completely fades away. Compare that with smokers using willpower, whose craving gets stronger the longer they delay having another cigarette.

Advantages of using Program 1

- Program 1 is most effective when the desire to smoke is still weak. By smoking when you feel like having a cigarette and using Program 1, you are extinguishing the learned association between the trigger and the reward.
- By using willpower and delaying lighting up, you are inevitably breaking down and rewarding yourself by smoking. Rewarding the behaviour makes it stronger and also strengthens the desire.
- By lighting up while the desire is still relatively weak, you can use Program 1 effectively. By controlling what you are thinking about and taking a deep inhalation of smoke, the Biocomputer learns the true consequences of smoking. This makes smoking unpleasant when the desire is weak and eventually makes the desire fade away completely.
- By using Program 1 effectively, you will spend the next few hours in a comparatively calm state. With willpower only, you will spend the next hour thinking about smoking in a state of moderate tension.

The more effectively you use Program 1, the less often you

will feel like smoking and the sooner you will quit smoking altogether.

James's progress

The techniques of this chapter can be illustrated by the experiences of James. On Tuesday, James felt that he couldn't stop smoking in the company of other smokers, as he would feel anti-social. The belief that not smoking in front of other smokers is anti-social was explored. It was pointed out to James that he should be aware of thoughts related to feeling anti-social amongst smokers. If he noticed such a thought, he was told to say to himself, 'Just because I'm with other smokers, it does not mean I need to smoke. Stopping smoking is not anti-social.' All the CBT techniques were explained to James and he felt confident that he could apply all of them. He liked the idea of learning to become a non-smoker and saw it as a challenge. He also felt that a gradual reduction of cigarettes was more realistic.

James felt excited about starting his new challenge. On day one, he put the rubber band on his cigarette packet, inserted the reduction card and started to take note of his triggers to smoke. James felt that he knew all of his triggers. However, he was surprised that, every time he smoked, it was related to a trigger and he discovered many new ones.

Summary

- Keep a rubber band on your cigarette packet so that you are unable to smoke automatically.
- Learn Program 1 (NURD) and automatically say it to yourself every time you smoke.
- Make a note of every cigarette you smoke on your Daily Reduction Cards from now on. At the end of each day enter your total consumption on your progress chart.

Day Two: Wednesday – regaining control from automatic pilot

One of the most important functions of the brain is to control essential life processes such as our breathing, blood supply, and digestive processes. The brain team and nervous system, together with the endocrine and immune systems, keep us ticking over, whatever we are doing, even when we are sleeping or unconscious. The brain enables us to perceive the environment, to learn and use language, to learn new skills, to imagine and create new things and to remember and understand our experiences.

The brain and nervous system are able to control things that are pre-programmed and to automatically perform all of those functions that keep us alive. Then other functions, which are 'optional extras', are added to the main bodily functions through the process of learning. This is where many of our problems begin.

Our physical and biological make-up has evolved over a couple of million years. We are built to live as hunter-gatherers but live as sedentary consumers. Our physical environment consists of the atmosphere, the land, and the water from which we draw sustenance. Unfortunately, much of our environment is now polluted with all kinds of unfriendly chemicals.

Our social environment consists of family, friends, neighbours, work colleagues and many other people with whom we have relationships. This has both emotionally supportive and less supportive elements. Contemporary urban living includes a diverse collection of hazardous activities and habits associated with our so-called 'lifestyle'. One of these is nicotine addiction, in which toxic fumes and chemicals are inhaled into our bodies as tobacco smoke.

Smoking has been represented by the tobacco industry as a 'cool' thing to do. For many generations of men and for the current generation of women, smoking has been a rite of passage into adulthood, but it is a habit that they have inevitably regretted when they are older. At first, the smoker has to put some effort into learning how to smoke a cigarette, inhale the smoke without coughing and look as if the process is enjoyable at the same time. In reality, while the young smoker may put on a front of trying to look cool, few people enjoy smoking on the first occasion of doing so. On the contrary, it is a highly unpleasant experience. Eventually, however, the smoker adapts to all of the unpleasant bodily sensations, a physical dependency on nicotine and a psychological dependency on the ritual developed and smoking automatically occurs whenever there is a desire to do so. That is how the smoking habit is acquired.

As the habit becomes more and more ingrained, smoking becomes an automatic response. The Chameleon part of your brain is actually in control of it. It is the automatic pilot. The lowest, most primitive part of your brain, normally helps you to survive and be healthy has been taken over by the deadliest habit known to humankind. Luckily, there are powerful methods to regain control from automatic pilot.

Pro-Cigarette Programs (PCPs)

While this analysis provides a general description of how people acquire habits and skills, there are large individual differences. On seeing a dog in the park, one person may go up to it and pat it, while another may avoid the dog because they feel frightened or insecure near dogs. The first person is programmed to react positively towards dogs because their experience with dogs suggests there is nothing to be frightened about, while the second person is programmed to react negatively towards dogs, perhaps because of an earlier frightening experience.

In similar fashion, as a smoker, you have been programmed to react positively towards cigarettes and the inhalation of cigarette smoke. In fact, you have many programs in your Biocomputer that are specifically designed to keep you smoking. Your primary task over the next few days is to discover as many of these PCPs as possible. Then you will replace them with programs that are beneficial to you. Impossible? Not at all.

The PCPs which encourage you to smoke have been drummed into your Brain Team by a large number of forces, most of which were external. Some of the main ones are:

- When you were in your teens, a desire to rebel against people who have tried to control your behaviour – parents, teachers, and other authority figures.
- The addictive properties of nicotine.
- Cigarette advertising making cigarette smoking appear cool.
- Peer pressure from smokers among your family or friends or other people you want to identify with.
- The idea that smoking helps you control your weight.

The addictive properties of nicotine become more powerful, the more that you smoke. As we saw in Part One, every time your nicotine level runs low and you top it up again by having a quick fix, smoking behaviour is strongly reinforced. Your smoking behaviour, including your desire to smoke, becomes linked to a whole host of stimuli in your immediate surroundings that act as triggers for your smoking. Whenever a trigger is present, your desire to have a cigarette increases. These associations have become deeply embedded in your mind by frequent repetition and reward. Every time you smoke a cigarette, your pleasure centres in your Chimp brain receive a shot of dopamine that reinforces a link between the desire to smoke, the sensations of smoking and aspects of your external environment. Eventually, those features of the situation which are repeatedly associated with smoking will become triggers which set off your desire to smoke. Triggers and PCPs have become a routine part of your life. For most of the time, you have been blissfully unaware that they are controlling your behaviour. They operate as automatically as your breathing, sitting in a chair, or walking. They just happen.

How A PCP Operates

Imagine the following scenario. You and some other smokers are watching television. One of the TV characters lights a cigarette. What happens in the room several moments after that? It is very likely that all the smokers will have reached for their cigarettes and will now have a cigarette burning. In spite of the regularity and uniformity of their actions, it is unlikely that they will be aware of what made them all have a cigarette at that particular point in time. In fact, it is a hidden program in each of their minds that has made them feel like smoking a cigarette whenever they observe someone else light up. If you ask any of the smokers why they lit up at that moment, the probable answer would be, 'I just felt like it.'

Here is what actually happened to the smokers:

PCP inside the Biocomputer – whenever anyone lights a cigarette, I will automatically feel like smoking.

Trigger – someone on television lights a cigarette.

Automatic response – I feel like smoking a cigarette.

As a smoker, you are programmed to respond automatically to many different trigger situations. You have almost no control over these automatic responses. Just as you are programmed to feel frightened when threatened with danger, you are programmed to feel like having a cigarette when presented with a situation that is associated with smoking in your mind.

Here is another example:

> PCP – *whenever I feel upset with someone, I will automatically feel like smoking.*

> Trigger – *husband/wife/partner comes home late from work and the dinner is spoiled in the oven.*

> Automatic response – *I feel like smoking.*

Each and every PCP needs to be individually deprogrammed so that in the future, when these situations occur, you will not automatically respond by smoking a cigarette. You need a strategy for discovering all of your trigger situations. Then, when you have identified each of them, you need a technique for responding differently. The process of discovering trigger situations will be helped by Program 2.

Program 2

Program 2 will make you aware of your smoking triggers. It is essential to have it firmly embedded in your mind. With a little bit of practice, every time you smoke you should be able to discover precisely what it was that triggered the feeling. The whole process can be remembered as 'WEST-D'.

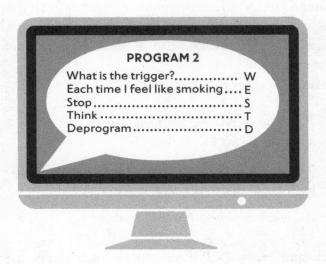

Every time you feel like smoking a cigarette, you should follow Program 2 (WEST-D – from the initials in the program). Every time you feel like having a cigarette, you acknowledge that one of your PCPs has been activated by a trigger. You must search for that trigger so that you can deprogram yourself. Once you have discovered what it was that triggered off the desire to smoke, you have a golden opportunity to deprogram the automatic response so that, the next time the situation occurs, you will be less likely to automatically light up. Methods of deprogramming are described later in this chapter.

You may have to go through the deprogramming process several times to get rid of each trigger. How often you need to deprogram will depend on how deeply embedded each program is and on how forcefully you deprogram it. However, in a very short time, you will find yourself thinking, Whenever that used to happen, I felt like a cigarette. Now, I never smoke in that situation! The realisation that you have changed your habits so easily is quite astonishing.

You probably have dozens of triggers, but all of the common ones are going to appear over the next few days. As and when they occur, you should deprogram them. Then, after you have done your WEST-D, you can light up, have a cigarette, and say Program 1.

A few triggers occur only on rare occasions, and they may not appear during the next few days. However, by the time one of them does appear, your general resistance to smoking will be a lot stronger and you will be able to cope with the trigger and not smoke.

On Stop-Day and afterwards, there will still be times when an old program is triggered, giving you the desire to smoke. Its effect may only last for a very short period, sometimes as short as a few seconds; but, even then, go through the same deprogramming process that you will learn in the next section. Make sure that, the next time the situation occurs, you won't feel like smoking. Remember that your mind contains the Biocomputer and, like an electronic computer, it has no will of its own. It is not fussy about what is programmed into it. It is as comfortable with Anti-Cigarette Programs in its memory files as it is with Pro-Cigarette Programs. To quit smoking for life, you should repeatedly deprogram your automatic responses every time you feel like smoking. Every time you feel that you want to have a cigarette, that is a signal for you to use Program 2.

Triggers

We are all programmed in our own individual ways and we all respond differently according to the individual events in our lives. However, we can all deprogram our automatic responses in the same way. Here is a list of some of the more common triggers:

- waking up in the morning
- finishing breakfast, lunch or dinner
- finishing washing the dishes
- sitting down in a chair to relax
- turning on the TV
- looking at a movie on a tablet or smartphone
- drinking a cup of tea or coffee, or some alcohol
- being in a bar
- feeling in a bad mood
- feeling rejected or lonely
- being with friends or people you like/don't like
- being offered a cigarette by another smoker
- seeing someone else light up
- seeing cigarettes on sale
- starting your car

- answering the telephone
- starting/finishing something
- preparing to go to bed
- after making love

Using Program 2, you will become very aware of which particular things trigger your desire to smoke. As soon as you realise what it is that is triggering the response to smoke, deprogram it! Keep a record of the triggers you have discovered on your Personal Trigger List. Update this list at regular intervals as you discover more triggers, and one by one you will be able to eliminate them.

Personal Trigger List

1
2
3
4
5
6
7
8
9
10
11
12
13
14
15
16
17
18
19
20
21
22
23
24

Deprogramming with words

There are two methods for changing your automatic programs:

1. Deprogramming by using *verbal commands*.
2. Reprogramming by using *imagery rehearsal*.

There are two major ways you can feed new information into your Biocomputer: through words and through images. Your Biocomputer is open to both channels of information. Before you can use images to reprogram new behaviour, you must first use words to deprogram the behaviour you no longer want. You can start using verbal commands for deprogramming right away. Reprogramming with images should be started tomorrow and is described in the next chapter.

Employ deprogramming as soon as you become aware that you are feeling like having a cigarette. Here's an example: imagine that you have just sat down in front of the television. You pick up your cigarettes. Reaching for the cigarettes is a signal for you to think of Program 2. You must go through the following **WEST-D** routine: **W – WHAT** is the trigger? **E – EACH** time I feel like smoking I must **S – STOP**. I **T– THINK** to myself: 'I feel like a smoke now. What is triggering that feeling?' You discover that it was because you had just turned on the TV and had sat down to watch a film. You realise that you always light up after you have switched on the TV and have sat down. It seems perfectly natural to reach for the cigarette packet in this situation.

Now that you have discovered what it was that triggered the desire to smoke, you should begin to **D – DEPROGRAM** it while you are still aware of it, so that it will not make you feel like smoking the next time you turn the TV on. To remove the programs that cause you to smoke, you need to feed completely new instructions into the Biocomputer. These new instructions must be specific, clear and to the point.

These verbal commands to your Biocomputer will deprogram the desire to smoke if you use them repeatedly and in an assertive, demanding and forcible manner. You must say the command as though you really mean it! By repeating the new instructions forcibly, you are giving your Biocomputer no option but to accept them. Be very clear about what you are trying to achieve. You are not trying to build up your willpower. You are ordering your Biocomputer to stop producing the automatic response 'I feel like a cigarette.'

Here is an example of how to carry out deprogramming. Imagine that you are having a cup of coffee. You feel like smoking a cigarette and use Program 2. You identify **What is the trigger?** You **Stop, Think, and Deprogram**. The last three steps are crucial. Here are some specific instructions that you could feed into your Biocomputer:

Wanting a cigarette now is just an automatic response to having a cup of coffee.

Just because I am having a cup of coffee, it doesn't mean I have to feel like smoking. The next time I have a cup of coffee, I refuse to automatically feel like smoking.

144

Whenever I sit down to drink coffee, I won't automatically think of having a cigarette. I won't be made to smoke just because I'm having a cup of coffee.

Your own verbal commands can of course say exactly what you want them to say. Be specific. Be emphatic. Be demanding. The language may sometimes be unprintable!

As soon as you feel like smoking a cigarette, you should go through the three main steps:

1. STOP (S)

Don't light up yet. Think of Program 2.

2. THINK (T)

Be aware that you are responding automatically. Ask yourself, 'What am I responding to?' When you discover what it is:

3. DEPROGRAM (D)

Begin to talk to your Biocomputer in a firm and demanding manner. Repeat the instructions over and over again to make a very strong impression on your Biocomputer. Be commanding. Be demanding. Be tough. Be a proper manager. Your Biocomputer will accept anything you program into it if you constantly and firmly repeat the idea you want it to accept.

The Chimp doesn't understand much English, but tries to listen in. The Chimp is not a good listener, but will know something is going on. It hears your stern tone of voice and will learn that you mean business. A new regime is taking over. The old rules are gone. Find another way to get your satisfaction, Chimp! It won't be nicotine.

This process needn't take up a lot of time. A few minutes spent repeating these ideas in your mind will pay dividends. By the very next day, you can expect to notice a situation when you would once have smoked, but this time you do not automatically reach for a cigarette. When you realise that this process is actually working and that your behaviour is changing quite dramatically, you will experience a great deal of satisfaction and enjoyment.

When you have gone through the three steps of 'WEST-D' and have told your Biocomputer not to respond by allowing Chimp to want a cigarette the next time, carry on with what you started to do. Drink a cup of coffee, begin watching television or whatever it was, while having a cigarette. It is vital that you smoke this time because you do actually feel like a smoke. But remember to say Program 1. The whole purpose is to deprogram an automatic response so that the feeling or desire to smoke stops coming automatically as a response to the trigger. So have the cigarette, but only after you have used the three steps and forcibly told yourself not to respond automatically next time.

As you continue to use Program 2 and the three steps, you will notice that you have lost the desire to smoke in each particular trigger situation. Smoke a cigarette afterwards (if you still feel like one) and use Program 1. Finally, don't forget to mark it on your Daily Reduction Card.

Why must new programs be repeated so mechanically?

Memorising programs and repeating them helps you to implant them deeply into your Biocomputer. Just reading them will not allow you to use them as active and effective tools to rid you completely of the need to inhale poisonous tobacco smoke. Memorise Programs 1 and 2 by rote repetition and use them from now on whenever you feel like a cigarette.

You will find that, by putting effort into memorising them, you can deeply embed them in your mind and they will soon function as automatically as the programs that keep you smoking. If they are well-learned, they will simply flash into your mind whenever you need them and you won't need to make any great effort to use them.

It is an extremely valuable exercise to list all the verbal commands that you discover. Typical examples might be:

The next time I wake up in the morning I will not automatically feel like lighting a cigarette.

The next time I have a cup of coffee I will not automatically feel like having a smoke.

The next time I put the washing in the washing machine I will not automatically feel like a smoke.

Most smokers have between twenty-five and thirty different triggers. If you reinforce the deprogramming process by writing down each verbal command, you will be able to read them through in the evening and have material you can use to begin reprogramming yourself with new desirable behaviour. As you continue to use these programs, you will notice that your daily consumption of cigarettes will fall without a great effort.

James's progress

James noticed many new triggers and used Programs 1 and 2 very consistently. He saw the whole experience as an interesting and enjoyable journey of discovery. By the end of Day Two, he had reduced his consumption to ten cigarettes.

His satisfaction and enjoyment with smoking had significantly reduced. He kept going, even though his confidence waned at times. Knowing that the progress so far was quite good, he kept a daily record of his progress on his chart and hung it over his computer at work. His work colleagues gave him their support – even those who also smoked. This was a great help to him. He looked forward to the weekend and to the idea that he would set a Stop-Day in the near future.

Summary

- Use Program 1 every time you smoke.
- Use Program 2 every time you feel like smoking.

- Deprogram yourself using the three steps. Every time you feel like a smoke, remember to STOP, THINK (What is the trigger?) and DEPROGRAM with strong verbal commands ('The next time I . . . I will refuse to smoke. Don't send me that smoking feeling. I'll smoke when I choose to do so.').
- Keep a list of your triggers.
- Make a list of your personal verbal commands.
- Keep a rubber band on your packet at all times.
- Complete your Daily Reduction Card and, at the end of the day, record the day's total on your Progress Chart.

6

Day Three:
Thursday – calming your
restless mind

As a smoker, you will probably agree that smoking often makes you feel calmer or relaxed. 'Feeling calmer' is one of the most common reasons given for smoking. Typically, smokers report feeling calmer while smoking. Smoking may help you to feel more at ease when you feel nervous or embarrassed. The ability to relax is seen as being one of the main benefits of smoking and many smokers smoke more when they are worried or 'stressed out'. Being able to relax provides a justification for continuing the habit.

You will learn how to make use of two of your natural abilities to make a breakthrough as a calm, happy and successful non-smoker. These abilities are your powers of imagination and of relaxation. Both abilities are universal, even among people who claim not to have them. Some people say they cannot 'see' things in their imagination for example. This belief is known to be false, however. Research over the last fifty years has shown that everybody dreams every time they have a night's sleep. When we dream, we are using our creative imagination. Dreams generate fantasies and alternative possibilities to those of everyday, waking reality.

You can dream and you can also generate images while you are awake. When you are daydreaming about something and your mind wanders to something pleasant, your mental imagery is fired into action. Why not learn to use your imaging ability to achieve something really healthy and useful, such as giving up smoking?

As you learn to use your creative imagination, you will discover that your ability to form vivid images depends upon your mental state. If you are feeling tense or upset, you may not be able to produce the images that you want or they may be very fleeting or poorly controlled. However, mental imagery becomes more vivid and easier to control when you are relaxed.

Imagery rehearsal

In this section I will show you how to use your powers of imagination to stop smoking now. You know from everyday experience that you can imagine future events and plan how to deal with them before they actually happen. On some occasions, these visualisations may be rather pessimistic and you will tend to imagine things going wrong. On other occasions, the images are optimistic and you will see how things could work out. People generally fall into one of these two types, pessimists (glass half-empty) or optimists (glass half-full). Some people move back and forth between these two styles. Which type are you?

For now, as team manager, you definitely need to put on a brave and positive face. Even if you have doubts about yourself as manager, now is not the time to show it. Be strong, be tough and be courageous.

Now that you have decided to give up smoking, use your images positively – that is, use your ability to rehearse situations where you will cope happily in the future without having a cigarette. You need to see yourself in a new light as a non-smoker.

The imagery method is very powerful indeed. Scientific trials have shown that the use of mental imagery to rehearse future performance helps golfers, athletes, and orchestra conductors to improve their skill. Patients have also been helped to cope with operations and to recover more quickly. You can learn to use these same mental processes to achieve your goal of becoming a successful non-smoker.

Everything that you imagine will be processed at different levels of consciousness. Your three inner brains will all register the power of your images. Even the Chameleon. One of the key features of your images is their *meaning*. Your images will suggest new programs for your Biocomputer that will influence your future thoughts, feelings, and actions. The Chimp will quickly see that you are seeing a different future. Even your primitive little Zee will see a different future. (More time for crickets.) A person's belief in what (s)he can achieve is a powerful determinant of what they actually do achieve. Thus, your images of yourself, of what you can and can't do and how you will feel as a result, all help to determine the outcome of your desire to stop smoking. Rehearsing images of yourself not smoking, and seeing yourself coping well with the more difficult triggers, will help these things to happen.

In order to actually become a beautifully balanced, calm and collected non-smoker, you must firstly be able to see this new you in your imagination. Try it now. Close your eyes and enter your private world of imagination. It is here that you make the decisions about the kind of person you would like to be and what you would most like to achieve. Try to see yourself as a happy and successful non-smoker.

Mentally rehearse a situation in which you would normally smoke a cigarette but see yourself coping without that cigarette. See yourself coping successfully, remaining perfectly happy and at ease without a cigarette. See it really happening: imagine as vividly as possible who else is there, what they are doing, how you are feeling, and how good it is not to be smoking in that particular situation.

The more you practise trigger situations in your imagination, especially while you are in a relaxed frame of mind, the more confidently you will be able to deal with these situations in real life. Eventually, all of your triggers can be completely eliminated.

Let's look at this process in more detail. Having started to deprogram your old smoking behaviour, your Biocomputer now has the capacity for some new programs and so you can reprogram new, non-smoking behaviour. PCPs can be replaced by Anti-Cigarette Programs (ACPs) and imagery rehearsal is one of the most effective ways of doing this. Your experience with Program 2 should have provided you with useful information about some of your principal triggers.

Some triggers should now be losing their power as a result of using Program 2. You may even have had a cup of tea or coffee without having an accompanying smoke, perhaps for the first time in many years! Others may be more resistant and require more repetition to be deactivated completely. Imagery rehearsal provides a useful method for building new behaviours and feelings to fill the gap left by smoking.

Make a list of triggers as they occur during the day or write out a list in the evening. Use your Daily Record Card to remind you exactly when you did smoke.

Imagery exercise

Allow about five minutes for this exercise. Sit in a comfortable chair, away from your TV, tablet, smartphone and other distractions. Try to become as relaxed as possible. You may even decide to try this last thing at night, before you go to sleep.

As you relax, think of one of your triggers. With your eyes closed, replay that particular scene as vividly as possible. But, this time, imagine that you don't actually smoke at all. Mentally practise the situation as you would really like it to have been. Imagine it as vividly as possible, pretending that you don't have a smoke. Repeat the image a few times, remaining as calm and relaxed as possible. When you can achieve a clear and vivid image of yourself coping calmly with the trigger but without smoking, you know that you will be better able to cope with that trigger in real life.

You should practise imagery rehearsal at least once each day for a few minutes to eliminate every trigger, one by one.

Calming your mind

We know that many people continue to smoke, despite being well aware that smoking is a lethal and unnatural activity. Why?

It is very common for people to become so concerned about their health that they try to give up smoking. Many do so. Many try and don't succeed. Some give up for an hour, a day, a few weeks, a few months, even a few years. But why do people start smoking again?

While you are in the process of deprogramming your old PCPs and replacing them with behaviour that is free from the need to smoke, your consumption of cigarettes begins to drop. This causes a problem that often defeats many would-be non-smokers. The problem has two parts:

1. Physically, you and your body are addicted to nicotine.
2. Mentally, your mind contains automatic programs that are triggering a desire to smoke.

The physical addiction

The addiction is easy to understand. Because you are smoking less, your body begins to react and demands its regular fix of nicotine. Because you don't feel like smoking so often, your body and brain team become desperate to get a supply of the drug nicotine. Your body (aided by your Chimp and Zee) begins to put pressure on you to smoke, to satisfy your addiction to nicotine. As you continue to deny your body the amount of nicotine that it is used to, your body responds by craving it, giving you pangs of urging and tensing up. The more you deny your body its fix, the more tense and stressed you will become. Having a cigarette will temporarily relieve the tension by satisfying the addiction. However, reducing your nicotine level tends to make you irritable and uncomfortable and it is at this stage that many smokers who are trying to stop smoking give in, rather than carrying on feeling so tense and miserable.

However, the tension in your body can be relieved in a far more satisfying and natural way than by smoking – by learning to relax. Instead of holding on to the tension that is building up in your body, you can learn how to let it go by learning to relax deeply. It is very simple to let tension flow out of the body, but most people carry tension around with them all day and, even at night, as they fall asleep, their fists are clenched and their muscles are tight. So many people suffer from headaches, ulcers, general irritability and nervousness, simply because they do not know how to relieve themselves of the everyday stresses and tensions built up in the body.

One of the most effective ways of releasing tension is by using meditation. This is a way of relaxing your mind and body very deeply and, by using this technique, you can reduce the desire to smoke by relieving the body of the tension that tends to build up when deprived of nicotine. A method of meditation is described in the next section of this book (see page 163). Meditation has always been a part of the *Stop Smoking Now* process. Recently, with the rise of mindfulness-based therapies, meditation has become quite trendy again, as it was in the 1960s. Roll over Beethoven!

The mental process

As you smoke less and less, the PCPs in your Biocomputer will be played over and over to tempt you to smoke. They do this in an extremely seductive and subtle way. Your Biocomputer mind, supported by all sorts of unsatisfied cravings and urges from Chimp, generates and invents the most amazingly convincing reasons why you should have a smoke. These reasons are often so cleverly thought up that, if you are not aware of what is happening, you will accept them and quite happily have a cigarette. The programs in the addicted and deprived part of the rational Biocomputer brain will start to generate *rationalisations*. These are delusory reasons to smoke.

In reality there are absolutely no good reasons to smoke, but the addiction programs are so subtle and creative that they will try to hoodwink the sensible part that wants to quit smoking. Unless you become fully aware of what is happening, these rationalisations will enter the mind quietly and sit there until you have got used to them. When you have almost automatically accepted one of them as true, you go and light up quite spontaneously. Clearly, you need a way of managing this.

Here is a typical example.

Let's assume that you have not smoked for the past two hours or so and you are sitting down with a cup of coffee. You realise that because you have been deprogramming yourself so well over the last couple of days, you didn't even feel like smoking when you sat down with your cup of tea or coffee. You are enjoying the fact that you are having your drink and not even feeling like smoking. Like a good manager, you have been giving verbal commands to your Biocomputer not to send the desire to smoke when you have a cup of tea or coffee and you have reinforced this by using imagery rehearsal in the evening to practise having a cup and enjoying it without smoking.

Now you pick up a magazine and hidden underneath is a packet of cigarettes. It is your favourite brand of cigarettes. Immediately another of your PCPs begins to play. You now feel like smoking. You think immediately of Program 2 and the three steps. You say to yourself, 'STOP. This is an opportunity to get rid of another trigger. THINK. What am I responding to? Obviously it's the sight of the cigarette packet. START DEPROGRAMMING.'

I refuse to obey that program.

The next time I see a cigarette packet, I will not automatically feel like a cigarette.

I absolutely refuse to be forced to smoke every time I see a cigarette packet.

I don't want to be a robot.

I don't want to react mechanically.

I don't want to be forced to smoke just because I see a cigarette advertisement.

Having finished giving your Biocomputer these stern verbal commands, you carry on reading your magazine. But, of course, the desire to smoke is still in you, the Chimp is getting restless and you are still thinking about smoking. Your mind seems obsessed with thoughts about smoking, and how much you would like to have a cigarette right now. Perhaps this sort of idea is in your mind:

'Well, I must say that I have been doing very well today. I haven't had a cigarette for two hours or more now. I'm making real progress. I didn't even feel like one with my cup of coffee! I went through that depro-gramming thing very well. Well, I don't have to stop until Stop-Day, so I may as well have one now. It's about time . . .'

Patting yourself on the back? Flattery? Yes, a very clever rationalisation, a very subtle trick to tempt you to smoke. It is so clever, that under the circumstances, you may very well go ahead and light up. However, it seems such a shame to think of rewarding yourself for being good with something that is actually denying you your wished for goal of stopping smoking. It is also slowly killing you!

You may also feel like this:

> *'I'm sick and tired of all this programming business.*
> *I feel confused about all the things I have to do. I'm*
> *losing my grip as a manager. My team's out of control.*
> *I'll just sit down and enjoy a smoke!'*

Would you like to know exactly how to deal with this type of rationalisation? It's such an obvious cop-out. Read on.

Program 3

Program 3 is used to counteract rationalisations. If you deny yourself a cigarette, the immediate response of your body will be to tense up until you give it another nicotine fix and your PCPs will start making up convincing reasons why you should light up.

Learn Program 3 by heart so that it will remind you to be aware of rationalisations and how to cope with them. This is how it goes:

PROGRAM 3

Each day is becoming easy.................E
And my mind is becoming calm.............A
So there are no good reasons to smoke...S
Yesterday's craving is gone...............Y

Spend time learning Program 3. It really is EASY. The EASY idea will occur to you whenever you begin to make up excuses or false reasons to smoke. There are no good reasons to smoke, but your mind will continue to make up reasons why you should. Program 3 helps make you aware of what is actually happening, and helps remind you what to do about it – calm your restless mind.

You will probably be well aware already of your tension and rationalisations. They can be counteracted effectively by the same method, the meditation technique. So saying Program 3 reminds you of the need to meditate as soon as possible. In fact, you should aim to do so for twenty minutes at least once every day.

How do I calm my restless mind?

- Simply being aware of what is happening, being aware that your Biocomputer will invent all sorts of reasons for you to smoke, and reasons why you shouldn't give up smoking will often turn off the rationalisation. By being aware of the process at work, you can to some extent gain conscious control over what you are thinking about.

- Learn to distract yourself. If you consciously let your mind dwell on how much you really want a cigarette, or let yourself be drawn into a contest between the desire to have a cigarette and your desire to resist smoking (willpower), the desire to smoke (the Chimp) will almost always win. Willpower is no match for the more powerful pro-cigarette programming. Rather than *fight* the desire to smoke, you can actually train yourself to distract your conscious attention away from smoking to something else. This is a particularly useful thing to do. If you can distract your attention with something else for only sixty seconds, the desire to smoke will pass. If you think that this technique of distracting your conscious attention away from smoking would be useful for you, practise it several times in your imagination. You will find that you are able to do it easily if you are willing to try it. It simply means consciously deciding to go and do something else, or occupy yourself with some activity for at least sixty seconds, until the desire to smoke has passed.

- Learn to meditate. This is the most powerful and effective way of stopping your mind from churning out rationalisations and reminding you that you feel like smoking. It is so simple to learn and to use and has the great benefit that your body becomes very deeply relaxed and you are able to unburden yourself of much of your tension. When you have learned to meditate, you should try and practise meditation for twenty minutes a day while you are giving up. The inner Chimp and Chameleon who are in constant search of novelty, cravings and urges and who are even more restless under the influence of your depleting levels of nicotine, will also calm down and relax when you meditate.

- If all else fails and you are unable to sit down for twenty minutes and meditate and unable to distract your attention for sixty seconds and you still feel like smoking, don't let yourself become more tense, upset or worried. Smoke a cigarette and say Program 1 to yourself while doing so! Smoke it deliberately and consciously, saying Program 1 in the same manner.

When smokers begin to cut down their consumption, they typically get caught up in a *stress-smoke spiral*. The less they smoke, the more tense or stressed they become. The more tense they become, the more they feel like smoking. This process can easily spiral a would-be non-smoker back into old smoking patterns again. In order to prevent this and to allow the deprogramming/reprogramming process to completely eliminate smoking, you need to intervene and stop the stress-smoke spiral. To relieve the tension being built up in the body, the smoker feels they must have a fix of nicotine which temporarily satisfies the urge to smoke. However, there are more satisfying and beneficial ways of relieving this tension and built-up stress. One of the most effective is meditation.

Meditation is an extremely simple and yet very valuable technique for producing profound relaxation and mental calm. Unlike tranquillisers, it has no side effects. Experiments have shown that the practice of meditation does indeed relieve stress and meditators tend to be more calm and relaxed than those who don't do it. It is also used to treat hypertension and drug withdrawal programmes. By following the instructions below, you will be able to:

- dramatically reduce your desire to smoke
- reduce your tension level and break the *stress-smoke* spiral
- deal more effectively with any stress from your work or family situation
- lower your blood pressure if it is higher than it should be
- really enjoy quitting smoking.

Learn the technique now and practise it every day until you have completely stopped smoking. You will find that by using it you will be able to get through the period when the body readjusts to not having a constant inflow of nicotine (the withdrawal period), without being irritable and emotionally upset. It requires just twenty minutes a day to be highly effective and is an enjoyable experience. The technique you will learn was developed by Dr Herbert Benson at the Beth Israel Deaconess hospital in Boston, USA. It is quite similar to transcendental meditation, publicised in the west by Maharishi Mahesh Yogi, who taught the Beatles how to meditate.

How to meditate

In its simplest, most basic form, meditation has four essential requirements:

A quiet environment

Ideally, you should choose a quiet calm room with as few distractions as possible. A quiet environment contributes to the effectiveness of the meditation by making it easier to eliminate distracting thoughts. When you do hear distracting noises, try not to let them upset you. Listen to them for a few moments, then gently go back to your meditation.

A constant mental stimulus

To shift your mind from worrisome or negative thoughts, there should be a constant mental stimulus which you can repeat silently. Since the relaxation effect is caused by the mind becoming calm, the repetition of a word (or mantra) is a way to break a train of distracting thoughts or stop your mind wandering. Your eyes should remain closed. Attention to your normal breathing rhythm is also useful and enhances the repetition of the mantra, a sound or word you focus your mind on. A good example is the word 'relax'. Say it over and over: 'Relax . . . Relax . . . Relax.'

A passive attitude

When distracting thoughts occur (as they will), they are simply to be disregarded, and your attention redirected gently to the repetition of the mantra. This is really very simple to do. As soon as you become aware that you are thinking about something else, let your attention drift back to the word, without worrying about it. Don't force things – let yourself enjoy it. You should not worry about how well you are performing the technique or worry whether or not you are doing it correctly, as then your attention will be on your worries rather than on the mantra. If you start to worry about how well you are doing, treat it as just another thought, and gently redirect your attention to the mantra. Adopt a 'let it happen' attitude. The passive attitude is perhaps the most important element for a relaxing meditation. Distracting thoughts may occur, but don't worry about them. They do not mean you are performing the technique incorrectly. When you realise that you are thinking about something else, just go back to repeating the word. Take it gently, and enjoy it.

A comfortable position

A comfortable position is important, so that there is no undue muscular tension at the outset. Your hands and arms are most relaxed when they are not crossed but lying comfortably in your lap. Allow your head to fall into a comfortable position. If you are lying down, you are more likely to fall asleep. You should be comfortable and relaxed in a sitting position.

Instructions

Before you begin to meditate, you should first read this section of the book, to help guide you into a relaxing meditation.

1. Sit quietly in a comfortable position.
2. Close your eyes and let your mind drift for a few minutes.
3. Deeply relax all your muscles, beginning at your feet and progressing up to your face. Keep them relaxed.
4. Breathe through your nose. Become aware of your breathing. Breathe naturally and normally. Listen to the sound of your breathing.
5. As you become more relaxed and your breathing becomes more steady, as you breathe slowly out, say, 'I am becoming relaxed,' silently to yourself. Breathe in, breathe out: 'I am becoming relaxed.' As you progress more and more into a relaxed state, you need only repeat, 'Relax,' each time you breathe out. Breathe in, breathe out. 'Relax.'

6. Continue to meditate for twenty minutes. You may open your eyes to check the time on a clock or watch near you. There is no need to set the alarm.

7. When you finish, sit quietly for several minutes, at first with your eyes closed, and later with your eyes open. Try not to stand up for a few minutes.

8. Do not worry about whether or not you achieve a deep enough level of relaxation. Maintain a passive attitude and let relaxation occur at its own pace. When distracting thoughts occur, just let them pass by, and return easily to repeating, 'Relax.' The whole process should be perfectly effortless. There is no need to strain or force things. The more you allow it to just happen, the easier and more successfully you will be able to meditate. With practice, you will find that your body can relax very deeply without any effort.

9. Practise this technique as often as you like, but make sure you do it at least once each day for about twenty minutes.

10. If you use this technique regularly, for twenty minutes a day, you will be able to break the *stress-smoke spiral* by releasing tension in your body and producing a calm state of mind. Your inner Chimp will be quiet and restful. It will be calmed.

The feelings associated with meditation are pleasurable. The more you enjoy it, the easier you will find it to relax deeply. Remember, just as each of us experiences anger, contentment and excitement, each of us has the capacity to experience the deep relaxation which meditation can provide.

AND YOU SAY THEY HELP YOU TO RELAX..

James's progress

By Thursday evening, James had smoked just six cigarettes so far that day and felt very pleased. He was thinking about not going out with friends on Thursday night, as he did not want to spoil his success. However, he had been advised to carry out normal everyday activities while trying to stop and he knew that going out for a drink on Thursday night was part of his weekly routine. So he went along to the pub with friends. His colleagues noticed the rubber band on James' cigarette packet and thought it was strange. James felt a sense of pride in describing this new method of quitting smoking. James used the card for the first cigarette that he smoked and recited the 'NURD' poem out loud in front of his colleagues. By his second cigarette, he was still using the rubber band. He did not note the following cigarettes on his card but he made a mental note and also told himself that the cigarettes were unpleasant and that he was losing the desire to smoke. He felt a genuine lack of desire to smoke that night. He smoked only eight cigarettes on Thursday.

Summary

- Use Program 1 every time you smoke.
- Use Program 2 every time you feel like smoking.
- Use Program 3 every time you invent reasons to smoke.
- You can calm your restless mind and reduce the tension in your body by using the meditation technique.
- You can calm your restless mind by becoming aware of what your mind is doing to you, and by distracting your conscious attention away from smoking.
- Don't get involved in a struggle between your desire to smoke and your desire to stop smoking. If you use willpower, you are relying on the Chimp to cooperate and you are very likely to lose. Use the subtle methods of meditation, relaxation and distraction.
- Complete your Daily Reduction Card and, at the end of the day, record the day's total on your Progress Chart.
- Enjoy the process of transforming yourself into a non-smoker!

Days Four, Five and Six: Friday, Saturday and Sunday – stopping unhelpful thought patterns

By this point, you should be well on the way to becoming a happy and successful non-smoker. If you have been following all of the procedures described in Chapters 4 to 6, your enjoyment of smoking will be considerably reduced and you will be smoking much less often than previously. However, it is still important that you continue to smoke whenever you feel like having a cigarette and that you say Program 1 ('NURD') to yourself while you smoke it. This eliminates the pleasure PCPs in your brain that tell you that smoking is enjoyable. It will remind your body of the true effects of smoking, which you experienced the first time you ever smoked.

It is essential that you also continue to Stop, Think, and Deprogram using Program 2 ('WEST-D'). This will eliminate the automatic way in which your smoking triggers make you light up every time they occur. You do not really want to be like a robot that automatically responds every time a smoking-related stimulus appears in your environment. Give yourself strong verbal commands that you will smoke only when *you* choose to do so. You do not simply have to smoke just because one of your triggers dictates that you must immediately have a smoke.

While Programs 1 and 2 will continue to work for you as you reduce your consumption, you should also allow time for Program 3 ('EASY'). Both imagery rehearsal and meditation take a little time, but they will both have a very calming effect on your mind. By now, you should have discovered the extra confidence that imagery rehearsal can bring you in reprogramming triggers. You should also have experienced the restful and relaxing effects that a few minutes' meditation can bring. The days that immediately precede Stop-Day are very crucial ones. These are the final days remaining to deprogram and reprogram your automatic triggers. The weekend days often present triggers that are different from those that you experience during the weekdays. Please be on the lookout, then, for some new triggers. You also need to be on the lookout for the subtle and seductive process of *rationalisation*. Rationalisation is represented by a process that I call the Argument Game. This is a fight that breaks out between the smoker inside you (the Chimp) and the non-smoker (you as the manager) who is trying to break free.

Smoker versus non-smoker

It is at this stage that imagery rehearsal and meditation can be most beneficial. This is because there will be some very strong rationalisations operating as the battle heats up between your two alter egos, the 'smoker' programs in the Biocomputer and you as manager, the 'non-smoker', who by now are definitely not seeing eye-to-eye. As predicted, the less you smoke, the more your consumption of tobacco goes down, the more desperate the smoker will become. The smoker programs are hell-bent on keeping you smoking and will try all kinds of psychological tricks to mask the true facts of the situation. Be prepared. Do not be conned as it tries to make smoking as attractive as possible to your conscious mind.

You know that smoking is a filthy, stinking, lethal habit. The smoker programs, on the other hand, tell you that smoking is a relaxing, satisfying and safe pastime. This internal 'Argument Game' continues almost constantly when you try to stop smoking by the use of willpower. In this CBT process, it has been one of the main aims to keep the use of willpower to minimum levels. However, the Argument Game continues, and it is essential that you learn how to win.

The Chimp and Zee are unable to take part in the Argument Game because they are illiterate and do not have language abilities. However, they provide background support by activating the Biocomputer's smoker programs with cravings, urges, and pressure to have a smoke.

According to the smoker, statistics are all a pack of lies — there is no evidence that smoking kills, it is purely statistical, nobody knows the cause of cancer and that's why there isn't any cure. The smoker will tempt you with all kinds of safe-sounding propositions such as, 'Go on, have one. You've only had three today and it's nearly bedtime. Have one now; it's only fair. You've done so well: you deserve a small reward.' Small reward, indeed! That's precisely the kind of nonsense that's kept smokers hooked for generations.

Another deceptive little ruse is 'It won't happen to me' syndrome. This is so well-known to psychologists that it has been given a special name: 'unrealistic optimism'. Everybody thinks that bad things won't happen to *them*, only to others. Of course, when something bad does happen, there is always the plaintive question: 'Why me?' The 'Not me/Why me?' illusion is practically universal in situations where people indulge in risky activities. Because they are doing it by choice, they feel a false sense of personal control over what the outcome will be. The fact is that lung cancer doesn't care why the victims' lungs are so crammed full of nasty toxic substances, it simply spreads and spreads until they require treatment or die.

In this chapter you will be guided to learn Program 4. This technique enables you to combat the rationalisations that your old pro-cigarette programming churns out: you can avoid getting involved in a power struggle between the two parts of yourself. You will learn how to anticipate some of the more common rationalisations. These are pseudo-reasons for having a cigarette, generated by your Biocomputer or by other smokers when they hear that you're trying to give up. This technique plays the Argument Game and gives you every extra advantage that it possibly can.

Program 4

Learn the following Program which will triumph over your inner smoker's last stand, the Argument Game.

The Argument Game

I will win. No you won't. Yes I will.
No you won't. Yes I will.
NO YOU WON'T! YES I WILL!
WON'T! WILL! WON'T! WILL!

Failure is not an option.

<u>N</u>O MATTER WHAT YOU SAY	N
THERE'S ONLY <u>O</u>NE WAY	O
TO PLAY THE ARGUMENT <u>G</u>AME	G
THERE ARE N<u>O</u> GOOD REASONS TO SMOKE	O

Learn Program 4 by heart (NO GO). It reflects the only sane attitude you can adopt as your Biocomputer starts to send you its Phoney Pro-Cigarette Arguments (PPCAs) – you just tell it NO GO!

Spend some time now reading through the ten PPCAs below and the ten counterarguments that go with them. Become familiar with the counterarguments so that you will be able to use them when needed. You should then be able to completely deflate these common rationalisations whenever they occur. Have the counterarguments ready so that you can say them either in response to your own Biocomputer or to other smokers. Knowing what to say can make all the difference. Non-smoker will be strengthened and smoker weakened by pure good sense, logic and scientific evidence! The rational use of information is rarely sufficient by itself as a method for stopping smoking. However, when you use cold logic in combination with your emotions and motivation, you have a total package that the smoker will find impossible to defeat.

Remember, there are absolutely no good reasons to smoke. Absolutely none! However, as the non-smoker takes over control, the smoker becomes even more subtle and devious. It may try to tempt you to stop following *Stop Smoking Now*, it may tell you that things are completely hopeless or that it is really too late to stop now because the damage has already been done or that you wouldn't get cancer anyway.

Ten phoney pro-cigarette arguments and their counterarguments

Rationalisations fall into four main categories:

1. Health
2. Social pressure
3. Economic
4. Personal discomfort

Study the PPCAs carefully. These, or similar, may be lurking in your mind right now. If you become aware of them, use counterarguments to eliminate them. This process is not a way of strengthening your willpower. Nor does it eliminate the need to continue with the programs that you have already started. Whenever you feel like a smoke, it is important to smoke, but use Programs 1 and 2 while doing so. The Argument Game is simply a way of noticing what is going on and tackling the phoniness of a smoker's case head on.

Health

Typically, these arguments emerge in the company of other smokers. They feel threatened when they see that you are giving up the habit and trot out arguments of the following kind:

Phoney pro-cigarette argument 1

All the evidence linking smoking with lung cancer is only statistical and has no relevance to me.

Counterargument 1

A series of reports published by the Royal College of Physicians in the UK has been categorical in stating that the simplest explanation of the evidence showing a relationship between smoking and lung cancer is *causal*. It is the view of all the major medical authorities that smoking cigarettes causes lung cancer. Smoking is known to be the largest single preventable cause of mortality and it accounts for one-third of all deaths in middle age (40 to 64 years). In addition to causing 90 per cent of all lung cancers, nearly all of which are fatal, smoking also produces cancer of the mouth, larynx, pharynx, oesophagus, pancreas, bladder, and other organs. In fact, smoking causes more premature deaths than AIDS, cocaine, heroin, alcohol, fire, car accidents, homicide and suicide put together! The more you smoke and the longer the time you spend as a smoker, the greater the risk of developing cancer or the many other diseases which are caused by smoking, such as chronic bronchitis, emphysema and coronary heart disease. The sooner a person stops smoking, the lower their chances of contracting one of these terrible diseases.

Phoney pro-cigarette argument 2

OK, I accept the evidence that smoking is harmful to my health but it's really too late now. The damage has probably already been done. There's little point in carrying on with this process as it only adds to my worries. I thought it was a good idea to try and give up when I first started, but it's too much effort, especially when it's probably too late to do anything anyway.

Counterargument 2

The Royal College of Physicians in the UK and the surgeon general in the US have shown a reduced risk of cancer among those who stop smoking. The risk of lung cancer could be cut in half within two or three years after cigarette smoking is stopped. The surgeon general has concluded that quitting smoking has immediate and long-term benefits, reducing risks for diseases caused by smoking and improving health in general.

'Within minutes and hours after smokers inhale that last cigarette, their bodies begin a series of changes that continue for years,' the Surgeon General Dr Richard H. Carmona stated. 'Among these health improvements are a drop in heart rate, improved circulation and reduced risk of heart attack, lung cancer and stroke. By quitting smoking today, a smoker can assure a healthier tomorrow.'

It is never too late to stop smoking. Stopping smoking at age sixty-five or older reduces a person's risk of dying of a smoking-related disease by nearly 50 per cent. Within a few days of smoking you will actually feel a lot better. You will feel fitter, breathe more easily, lose the 'frog in your throat' and regain your senses of smell and taste that were partly shut off by smoking. You will also smell a lot cleaner and fresher, without the stink of stale tobacco smoke on your clothes, hair, and skin. The sooner you give up, the sooner your physical health will return to normal levels.

Recent research has shown that giving up smoking has a positive effect on reducing the risk of coronary heart disease (CHD), regardless of age. The relative risks of CHD were compared in never-smokers, former smokers and current smokers in men of two age groups, fifty-one to fifty-nine and sixty-five to seventy-four. In both age groups there was a consistent decrease in CHD incidence as smoking experience decreased and former smokers in both age groups showed lower incidence of CHD than smokers. Thus, quitting smoking, even at an advanced age, results in a reduction of risk. It is never too late to quit smoking.

Phoney pro-cigarette argument 3

OK, I accept that I'll be healthier physically, but I depend on cigarettes to perk me up, to help me relax and to concentrate. I won't be able to perform as well when under pressure if I can't have a cigarette.

Counterargument 3

It is true that smoking is perceived as a stimulating and relaxing thing to do. But, however good you may feel when you have a cigarette, you know that this is one of the main effects of the dependency that you have built up. By deprogramming your desire to smoke and by learning new ways of relaxing, you will be able to cope with pressure and stress much better without the need to have a smoke. You will also be able to concentrate on what you are doing without the need for a cigarette.

A cigarette only seems necessary at present because your central nervous system has become used to having regular supplies of nicotine. You are a cigarette junkie who needs a regular hit of nicotine. As a smoker you perceive that smoking helps alleviate your negative mood states, but the evidence from the Royal College of Physicians suggests that 'the only negative mood state so alleviated is that resulting directly from the nicotine dependence itself. Thus, the nicotine in tobacco relieves nicotine–withdrawal symptoms, but does not have mood enhancing properties in non-addicted individuals. If anything, the experience of being addicted to tobacco appears to add to, rather than relieve, stress in the everyday lives of smokers.' In other words, you are rationalising and justifying your smoking, using a false argument. Smoking makes you want to smoke more. It is only calming because you are addicted.

Social pressure

Phoney pro-cigarette argument 4

Other smokers, or even your own Biocomputer, may churn out the following: 'I've heard about people who've been smokers and lived to ninety and then there are others who've never smoked and die in their forties. You die when you die and that's all there is to it. At least you may as well be happy while you're alive.

Counterargument 4

People who use these sorts of arguments ought to study Counterarguments 1 to 3. Try to avoid arguments with other smokers. Simply tell them, 'No, thanks. But you go ahead if you want to.' Social pressure takes many different forms. It was probably social pressure that helped to get you smoking in the first place. Don't let these pressures affect you again, now that you are aware of the facts about smoking. If others want to smoke, that is really their affair, and you certainly do not need to keep them company. Tell yourself (and your Biocomputer) that you will make a point of refusing when others put pressure on you to smoke. Compared to ten or fifteen years ago, the tables have turned and there is a lot of pressure on smokers to stop smoking. As an almost non-smoker, you can therefore easily take the upper hand. Be assertive and say, 'No, thank you,' every time you're offered a smoke by another person. It won't be long before all your smoking friends will want to follow your example and give up too. Be proud, firm, and confident, and always say, 'No.'

Phoney pro-cigarette argument 5

In spite of Counterargument 4 above, your Biocomputer or another smoker, may eventually push you to the limit and say, 'Go on, have one. One cigarette can't do you any harm.' Initially, you may even feel like giving in by thinking or even saying, 'That's right. Just one can't make much difference. I'll just have this one.'

Counterargument 5

How dangerous the Argument Game is becoming! Especially so if you start agreeing with that devious inner smoker and all its phoney arguments. Don't be a fool! This is the oldest trick in the book. When you stop to think about it, every smoking habit consists of one long series of 'just one' cigarettes. When you find the Argument Game turning into the 'Just One Game', you know you've still got some serious deprogramming to do. If you do have 'just one', remember always to say 'Program 1'. And, every time you feel like one, use the 'WEST-D' procedure at the same time.

Another version of the Just One Game has already been mentioned. This is when your Biocomputer congratulates you for being so clever in cutting down and then suggests that you deserve a cigarette as a reward! This is surprisingly common, so be on your guard at all times. The old smoker programs would love to catch you out because the smoker realises that 'just one' cigarette wouldn't be just one at all, but a whole new series of cigarettes and then the full-blown habit would quickly become re-established. You wouldn't fall for this one now – or would you?

Phoney pro-cigarette argument 6

Somebody you are close to may be a smoker and perhaps

you're trying to stop, but they are not. The person ('X') says to you, 'Come on, have a cigarette.' Or you watch them smoking and your Biocomputer says, 'Go on, have one. If you don't, X will start sulking. No point in creating a fuss. You'll get along together if you don't rock the boat by refusing to smoke.'

Counterargument 6

However appealing this tugging at your heart-strings may be, it is of course a false reason for smoking. Your eventual success at giving up will provide an excellent incentive for your partner to follow suit. Ideally, both of you will be giving up at the same time. Never smoke because somebody else does. There are no good reasons to smoke.

Economic

These arguments are perhaps the weakest and flimsiest of them all. However, your Biocomputer, under the influence of your pro-cigarette programming, will try any argument at all to try to get you smoking again.

Phoney pro-cigarette argument 7

Your Biocomputer says, 'You gave up smoking because you thought you'd notice it in your pocket. But you haven't really saved much cash. What have you got to show for it so far in hard cash? For what you save, it's hardly worth the effort to give up.'

Counterargument 7

Calculate your own personal life expenditure on cigarettes. Some people have used what they would formerly have spent on cigarettes to buy something they have wanted for a long time. One woman used the fifty pounds she used to spend per week on cigarettes to pay off a washing machine and dryer (and she still had twenty pounds extra in the hand). Think how much you will save.

Rosemary used to smoke a packet of cigarettes a day before she stopped. In 2016, just before she stopped, she was spending £9.40 per day or £65.80 per week, on cigarettes. Multiplying this by fifty-two gives a total of over £3421 per year. Since Rosemary was paying tax at twenty-five pence in the pound, smoking was costing her around £4500 per year of gross income.

Make your own calculation. See how much smoking was/is costing you:

Cost per day: _____

Cost per week: _____

Cost per year: _____

Now decide what you'd like to do with your extra money. Think of something that you could purchase. How about some new clothes, a special trip, new DVD player, camcorder, dishwasher or a surprise present for someone special? Work out now what you will do with the money you save by continuing life as a non-smoker.

Personal discomfort

For many people, the discomfort caused by restlessness, depression or ill-tempered moods and nervous habits is a big problem. These discomforts are withdrawal symptoms. Some people find that their consumption of snacks, such as nuts, ice cream and soft drinks, increases when they cut down on cigarettes. Your Biocomputer can easily manipulate you into this vulnerable situation. Beware of threats about what might happen to you when you stop.

Phoney pro-cigarette argument 8

Your Biocomputer may suggest, 'Think how terrible you will feel if you stop smoking.'

Counterargument 8

For the first few days, or at most weeks, the smoker who does not relax may well feel moody and ill at ease. But, however you feel at this stage, it is infinitely more bearable than cancer, bronchitis, or emphysema, when your lungs actually erode. However awful, irritable, or ill-tempered you may feel, the long-term gains are well worth the effort. Your Biocomputer may try and convince you that you are losing control and that to start smoking again is your only solution, your only way of returning to normal. These are powerful and persuasive arguments, but they are wrong. Smoking is certainly not normal, and you are gaining control, not losing it, when you quit smoking.

If you allow yourself to relax deeply by meditating and use mental rehearsal to reprogram the rest of your triggers, you can avoid the discomfort of built-up tension during the withdrawal stage.

Phoney pro-cigarette argument 9

This argument is very similar to no. 8, so watch out for it! Your Biocomputer (or an interested bystander) says, 'If you stop smoking you will gain unwanted weight. If you carry on smoking, you will stay slim.'

Counterargument 9

Your Biocomputer is trying to flatter you by appealing to your vanity. But, rest assured, if you put on a few extra pounds now, it will be worthwhile. First, stopping smoking will give you a happier, healthier life in the long run. Second, in a few weeks you will be able to normalise your weight without using smoking as a form of weight control. Your long-term health is surely more important than a little extra weight in the short term. At the moment, smoking is the problem you should focus on. You can tackle the weight problem, if it develops, later; see Chapter 10 for more details.

Phoney pro-cigarette argument 10

Your Biocomputer says, 'You have already cut down on your consumption. That's good enough. There's no need to go any further. Your lower daily consumption is a fine achievement. Well done. Have a cigarette. Just one cigarette won't do you any harm'.

Counterargument 10

The 'Just One Game' is a crafty trick played by your Biocomputer trying to assert the last remnants of its control. Your PCPs have all but disappeared and they are desperately trying to regain their lost control. Your goal is to give up smoking completely. You know all the reasons. If you pretend you are satisfied with yourself by continuing to smoke at your current daily level, then think again. Your smoking will easily creep up to the original level; your Biocomputer and pro-cigarette programming will have beaten you and, once more, you will be a smoker.

The path is clear and obvious: never, ever succumb to an argument which tells you to give in. You will not be content until you have given up smoking completely and forever.

This list of Pro-cigarette arguments and counterarguments could be extended. By now you should be able to recognise the Argument Game and be well prepared to deal with any pro-cigarette argument that comes along. Remember, there are absolutely no good reasons to smoke.

Systematic sensitisation using the eight steps

You are now very close to Stop-Day, the day when you will not smoke. If you have been following this therapy process carefully, you will have most of the automatic responses you have experienced as a smoker under your control. On Stop-Day, you will find it easy to maintain your self-control and do what you consciously desire – not to smoke.

However, you are well aware of the power of the programs in your mind that continue to put pressure on you to smoke. There will be times when you are tempted to have a cigarette. There will be situations which trigger the desire to smoke that you have been unable to deprogram because they have not come up yet. There may be times on Stop-Day or afterwards when your Biocomputer (under the influence of a PCP) will suggest that you 'Just have one puff' or 'Just have one last one' or 'Just have a few puffs to see if you really do or don't like smoking any more'. It could play the Just One Game for some considerable time.

The next section provides a further technique to help you finally destroy your dying PCPs. You should be able to calmly resist having that 'just one', even if you are really tempted. Your success is obviously going to be linked to being able to stay calm and in control of yourself without having to force yourself by using your willpower. By using willpower, you open up the conflict between two competing desires: the desire to smoke, which is your inner Chimp, and the desire to stop smoking, which is you the manager. It is usually far easier to smoke than to fight. You must constantly be on your guard and employ more powerful methods of defence than argument alone. The technique that follows is a way of sensitising you to the true effects of smoking and will remind your body of the true effects of smoking.

To use the sensitisation technique to full advantage, you should read the next section right through. Use your creative imagination to link each step with the visual image suggested. Treat this technique seriously and follow the instructions exactly. You may find the imagery rather disturbing. However, the descriptions accurately reflect the realities of smoking. By avoiding these situations, you are closing your eyes to what actually happens when people smoke. Have a packet of cigarettes handy before you read on. Be encouraged by the fact that this packet could be your last!

The Eight Steps

Please fully acquaint yourself with the Eight Steps. Although it is possible that you are not consciously aware of them, you go through them every time you smoke. Take a few minutes now to learn the Eight Steps.

STEP 1   Pick up the packet, open it and look at the cigarettes inside. Be aware of how the cigarettes look. Do it now.

STEP 2   Take a cigarette out of the packet, but don't put it in your mouth yet. Become aware of what it feels like to hold the cigarette between your fingers. Roll it around a little to really get the feel of it.

STEP 3   Put the cigarette in your mouth. You should become aware of the sensation between your lips. Do it now. Really try to experience the shape and the feel of the cigarette in your lips.

STEP 4   Now light a match or lighter. Bring the flame up almost to the end of the cigarette, but don't light it. You will actually feel the heat of the flame on your face and fingers. Become aware of the heat from the flame on the surface of your skin.

STEP 5   Now light the cigarette and inhale a puff of smoke. Be aware of the smoke you inhale.

STEP 6   Now exhale the smoke from the first puff. Feel it and see it coming out of your mouth.

STEP 7   Smoke the cigarette through. Of course, don't forget to use Program 1 as you smoke it.

STEP 8   Stub out the cigarette in the ashtray. This time, stub it out rather more forcefully than normal. You are aware of the pressure on your thumb or fingers as you stub it out.

Linking the eight steps to images

In this section we will use the eight steps and link an image to each. As you read this section through, really try to visualise each situation. The association will be so powerful that, each time you go to have a cigarette, you will automatically think of the linked image. The association will be so strong that you will have an automatic warning device to help you overcome the temptation to have a cigarette.

Remember that the desire to smoke is only a trick of the mind conjured up by your Biocomputer to force you to administer yourself a fix of nicotine. By using this technique, you will have a whole series of warnings that will remind you that you are being continuously tricked into smoking. You will reprogram your Biocomputer with new anti-smoking programs to replace the diminishing traces of your old pro-smoking programs.

Be prepared now to smoke a cigarette in your mind. You are going to create a fantasy experience by imagining that you are lighting a cigarette while you are reading. As you read the script, imagine that you are going through the procedure of lighting and smoking a cigarette. Do this as vividly and realistically as you possibly can.

STEP 1   Your packet of cigarettes is lying beside you. You decide to have a cigarette. You pick up the packet and open the lid. As the lid opens and you look into the packet, you see not cigarettes but the dead bodies of people who have died from lung cancer. Imagine that each cigarette is one dead body wrapped in a white sheet. The cigarette packet you are holding is a coffin full of cancer victims who died because they were cigarette smokers.

STEP 2   Now imagine that you take a cigarette out of the packet. You are aware of its shape. It turns into a bottle of lethal poison that you are going to administer to yourself. It is a paper container filled with dozens of cancer-producing chemicals. You are now going to take this brew of lethal poisons into your system – a form of slow-motion suicide.

STEP 3   Imagine that you now put the cigarette into your mouth. You are aware of it between your lips.

You feel the roundness of the filter; you are very aware of the unpleasantness this causes in you because it almost seems as if there is a cancerous growth on your lip. You can feel it on your lip growing and spreading. It is a cancer caused by cigarette smoking, a cancer which occurs substantially more often in smokers than in non-smokers. You can feel it between your lips.

STEP 4 Now imagine that you light a match or your cigarette lighter. You look at the flame, at the fire and, as you bring it closer to your face, you become very aware of the heat on the surface of your skin. You can feel the heat, the fire on your face. You think to yourself, this is the fire I am going to take into my lungs. This is the burning fire that will destroy me.

STEP 5 Imagine that you light the cigarette. Imagine that you are very tiny and that you are standing inside your own mouth. You can see your teeth, tongue and, as you look around, you become aware of your lips. Between your lips you can see the round end of the cigarette sticking through into your mouth. You hear a rumbling sound as your chest, far below, begins to expand and you begin to breathe. As your chest expands, you suddenly see the thick grey-white smoke pour out of the end of the cigarette. It is thick and dense. It pours into your mouth, and as you watch, you can see the tiny droplets of thick brown, oozing tar being deposited onto your teeth; you can see the dense white smoke pour down the opening at the back of your mouth into the throat. It pours, rushes down, down through your larynx, down the tubes which lead into your lungs. You can see the tiny hairs covered with mucus on the inside of the tubes freeze. Their function as the dirt removal system of the lungs is paralysed. You can see the dense smoke enter the tiny air sacs of your lungs. You can see the droplets of tar being deposited on the delicate tissues of your lungs. You are very aware that the whole atmosphere inside your breathing system is filled with poisonous gases. Hydrogen cyanide – one of the deadliest gases known, used as a poison gas during World War I. Nitrogen dioxide – the amount of this gas in one cigarette can produce an acid strong enough to burn holes in a nylon stocking; this is the gas that may cause emphysema, where the tiny air sacs burst and collapse in the body's struggle to obtain oxygen and get rid of carbon monoxide. Carbon monoxide – a gas which is quickly absorbed into the bloodstream and is swiftly transported to the brain, where it begins to cause substantial impairment of its function. It starts to impair your vision, judgement and attentiveness to sounds. The smoke, the gases: you are suffocating, you are suffocating!

STEP 6   You are now aware of movements in your diaphragm, which now begins to push upwards, to push the smoke out of the lungs. You feel the movement of the diaphragm; it is almost the same sensation you feel when you are sick and begin to vomit. As the diaphragm pushes upwards, the smoke begins to spew out of your mouth; it is as if your body can no longer tolerate the poisonous fumes. It is forcing them out, almost vomiting them out.

STEP 7   You continue to draw on the cigarette and the smoke continues to pour down your lungs. You are very aware of the effects of the smoke on your body. You are reciting Program 1 to yourself. You can feel the heat of the smoke on your tongue, feel the harshness on your throat; you can feel your heart pumping harder than normal because, from the first puff, the drug nicotine began to speed it up and put it under strain. You can feel the strain on your heart. You continue to smoke the cigarette down to the hot, bitter end.

STEP 8   You feel ill; you feel the heaviness, the thickness, the aching in your head. You can tolerate it no more – you cannot, you *will* not tolerate it any more. You stub it out hard, killing it before it kills you.

If you feel at all tense or upset for any reason after reading this section, make use of the strong feelings you have to continue deprogramming yourself of the desire to smoke. Say to yourself, 'I have had it with smoking! I just don't want to smoke any more. I refuse to be pushed into something that I don't really want to do.' Spend a few minutes now, giving your Biocomputer some very strong *verbal commands* about how you want to see yourself. Do this now! It is worth the effort to spend a few moments talking to yourself in a strong and definite way. When you have finished giving yourself some strong verbal commands about how you want to be completely free from cigarette smoking, take some time to relax. It will be beneficial to spend twenty minutes meditating, just letting the tension flow out of your body. Sit back and let yourself completely relax.

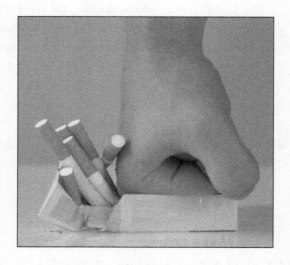

Give your Biocomputer strong verbal commands.

Planning your Stop-Day

Choosing the right day for Stop-Day is crucial. Stop-Day and Stop-Day Minus One are both crucial days. Another name for the Stop-Day is D-Day. I am able to say with some conviction that the planning of Stop-Day is absolutely crucial to its success. Just as more than 150,000 courageous people fought on the beaches of Normandy to free the world from the scourge of Hitler's Nazism on D-Day, 6 June 1944, you and thousands of others can be free from the smoking scourge by fighting a carefully planned D-Day of your own. Like our heroic forebears led by Churchill and Eisenhower, you need to decide which day is to be your D-Day, as much in advance as possible. At the very latest this will be during the twenty-four-hour period immediately before. If you decide on one day but the weather is stormy (as it was way back on 5 June 1944), you can decide to delay it to another day when you will be confident enough to weather the seas that will release you from the smoking habit.

For example, if you originally planned to make Stop-Day a Monday, then you may decide to make Tuesday your Stop-Day. What you should not do is decide to make Tuesday your Stop-Day on Tuesday. This is because you won't be sufficiently prepared and part of Tuesday will already have gone. Stop-Day is a complete twenty-four-hour period, starting at midnight and it should be planned at least twenty-four hours in advance.

Here are a few guidelines, based on the experience of several thousand people who have already succeeded.

- Look at your Progress Chart. This will tell you exactly how well you are doing. Provisionally choose a day when you can be reasonably sure that your consumption will only be one to three cigarettes on Stop-Day Minus One. The trend could be something like this:

  - Tuesday: 24 cigarettes
  - Wednesday: 13 cigarettes
  - Thursday: 7 cigarettes
  - Friday: 4 cigarettes (provisionally set Stop-Day for Sunday)
  - Saturday: 2 cigarettes (confirm that Stop-Day will be Sunday)
  - Sunday/Stop-Day: 0 cigarettes.

- When you arrive at Stop-Day Minus One, hopefully your cigarette consumption will be right on target and you will smoke only one to three cigarettes that day. In that case, your Stop-Day should be confirmed for the next day. Make a deliberate, conscious decision, taking all factors into account. You should make the decision before midnight.

- Your consumption immediately prior to Stop-Day should be the main factor, but it is not the only one. Please also take into account what you will be doing that day. Choose a day when you know things will be reasonably 'normal'. Choose a day when you feel confident that you can and will succeed. Not everybody progresses as smoothly as shown in the example. Some people reduce their consumption and then have a bad day or two, when their smoking increases to higher levels again. In this case, follow the original procedures again, but apply more concentration to the de- and reprogramming while using Programs 1 to 4. Nobody who applies Programs 1 to 4 consistently should fail to reduce their cigarette consumption to zero. When your consumption has fallen to one to three cigarettes, which it should do within five to ten days, then you know that your Stop-Day has arrived.

James's progress

On Friday James smoked only six cigarettes. He went through the NO GO procedure and discovered a lot of rationalising going on. More triggers also appeared that had not appeared earlier in the week. He realised that the weekend might bring some surprising new triggers and so he doubled his efforts to become aware of his inner thoughts and feelings as these seemed more relevant now than earlier in the week.

James learned the Eight Steps and, when he smoked, he not only used Program 1 (NURD) but he imagined the unpleasant images of each of the Eight Steps of smoking. James set aside a twenty-minute quiet period on Saturday and Sunday for meditation. James gained a lot from this as he felt more calm and relaxed.

On Saturday James smoked five cigarettes and on Sunday smoked only two cigarettes. He decided to make Tuesday his Stop-Day. On making the decision James felt he was making a new start to his life. He resolved never to smoke again after midnight on Monday.

Summary

- Every time you smoke, think of the Eight Steps and the eight images that go with them.
- Continue using Programs 1 to 3 whenever or wherever the need arises.
- Meditate every day and practise mental rehearsal every night before you go to sleep.
- Become aware of all your Biocomputer's rationalisations. Play and win the Argument Game (Program 4: NO GO).
- Plan your Stop-Day carefully. Set yourself a target date. Confirm it the day before, when your consumption should be no more than one to three cigarettes. A well-executed Stop-Day will free you from the scourge of smoking forever. Be heroic on your Stop-Day!
- Complete your Daily Reduction Card, and, at the end of the day, record the day's total on your Progress Chart.

8

Surviving Stop-Day and starting your new life as a non-smoker

Using the techniques in the last few chapters, you are now well equipped with some powerful methods for stopping smoking. Using these methods should be enough for most smokers to beat the smoking habit forever. This chapter gives you further techniques to finalise the process of quitting over the weekend and to help you to survive your Stop-Day.

This chapter should be consulted whenever you feel like a cigarette from Stop-Day onwards. If you do get the desire to smoke, there will always be something you can do about it. This chapter provides you with a variety of techniques to prevent any further smoking, however sorely you may be tempted. In Part Three, you will find details of other, longer-term ways of coping.

Here is a list of things that you can do on Stop-Day to rid yourself of any remaining desire to smoke:

Progressive relaxation of your whole body

Sit in a comfortable chair, with both feet resting on the floor and your hands in your lap. Close your eyes and, starting at your feet, gradually move up through your body, relaxing all of your muscles. Do this for your feet, calves, thighs, buttocks, back, shoulders, stomach, chest, arms, hands, fingers, neck, face, mouth, eyes, cheeks and forehead. Think of each area and say to yourself, 'My arms are relaxing, my arms are relaxing' or 'My face is relaxing, my face is relaxing.' Sit for a few minutes, doing this, and you will find that the physical relaxation of your body flows through into your mind.

This technique of deep relaxation can be most beneficial. You will be able to use it to change your self-concept to that of a non-smoker and experience a calm and confident feeling that you have crossed the boundary from being a smoker to becoming a non-smoker. Your mind will be freed from distractions and be more ready to accept new ideas and information. You will discover that your confidence is growing so that you will be able to strengthen your new non-smoking behaviour.

Meditation exercise

Do this at least once on your Stop-Day; preferably early in the day before you encounter too many people, situations, or events. This exercise will relax you deeply and leave you feeling more calm and confident. It will strengthen your resolve and determination not to smoke. It will further weaken your automatic responses to triggers when you encounter them during the day. Your mind will become calm and you will be able to cope better with any remaining anxiety, stress and strain that may bother you on Stop-Day. You should do this later in the day as well, if at all possible: in the afternoon, perhaps, or in the evening. You will calm your restless mind. Chimp and Zee will enjoy it too!

Fantasy techniques

There are many of these and you will be able to construct some of your very own using the ideas listed below. The basic principle is to imagine pleasant scenes and situations which you know would make you feel perfectly calm and relaxed. For example, sit in your most comfortable chair, close your eyes, and imagine that you are lying on a beautiful beach in some exotic place in the warmth of the afternoon sun. Create a fantasy which allows you to feel at ease and comfortable. Let the pleasant scene unfold and, as it does so, you will feel very calm and relaxed.

Imagery rehearsal

Follow the procedures described in Chapter 6. While relaxed, imagine yourself in one of the trigger situations that you most fear. See it, hear it and feel it with all the power of your imagination. Then imagine coping with this situation perfectly well without a cigarette. Remember, the more clearly and vividly you can imagine yourself coping with the problem situation, the more easily you will be able to manage it in real life. Repeat with other triggers, until you feel that you are capable of treating each of your triggers with complete detachment.

Body imagery

Sit down and close your eyes. Imagine you can actually see your blood flow. Imagine your skin has suddenly turned transparent and you can see the flow of blood in your body, warm and cosy, bathing the muscles with a soothing relaxing effect. Imagine the warmth creeping up from your feet. Feel how comfortably warm your body is getting. Warmth in your legs, your abdomen, your chest. Warmth in your face. Feel the flow of warmth moving down your back. Continue for as long as you wish, then open your eyes.

Rag doll imagery

Sit down for a few minutes and close your eyes. Imagine you are a rag doll – a floppy, soft, rag doll that just collapses when dropped. A rag doll that straggles all over the place when you throw it down. Imagine that's what you are now. Throw your arms and legs out and let them just flop. Limp and floppy. See your rag doll muscles. They're made of wool. Limp, floppy wool! It is a ridiculous thought, but stay with it for a few minutes. Visualise your muscles dropping down there like a handful of wool. Repeat these images until you feel perfectly relaxed. Open your eyes.

Elevator imagery

Sit down and close your eyes. Imagine that you are on the twentieth floor of a tall building. Imagine yourself going to the elevator. See yourself pressing the call button. See the elevator doors opening. Get into the elevator; see the doors closing. Now try and remember the feeling or sensation you get when an elevator begins to move down. Imagine yourself moving slowly and smoothly downwards. See the numbers light up as you go down. Say to yourself, 'As I go down, I feel more relaxed.' Say it every time you pass a floor. When you reach the ground floor, get out of the elevator and relax for a short while. Then get back into the elevator and swiftly return to the twentieth floor and open your eyes.

Create a space

This technique can be used at any time, whether you are with people or by yourself. It is extremely useful to be able to create a space in situations where you can't leave to sit down and relax. This is how to create a space:

1. Select a time and place when you were particularly happy and relaxed. It may be a pleasant childhood memory, something that happened on your last trip or the last time you were at the beach or in the countryside. The most important point is that you were feeling happy and relaxed, having a good time and enjoying yourself.

2. If you can't think of a real experience, then make one up. Make it a beautiful experience. Perhaps it is in the mountains. Perhaps it's a very special dream.

3. You must experience your situation. Try to remember or make up as many details as possible. Try to answer the following questions in your mind:

- Where are you?
- What time of day is it?
- What are you doing?
- Who is with you?
- What are you wearing?
- What are you touching?
- What colours are there?
- What can you see to the right and to the left?
- If you turn around, what can you see?
- Are you aware of any smells? (Flowers? The sea? The forest?)
- What is the weather like?
- Are you aware of any sounds? (Waves, birds, people, the wind?)
- Imagine how you are feeling.
- What were you doing half an hour ago?
- What are you likely to be doing in half an hour's time?

4. Now that you have built up your fantasy in detail, you can begin to use it. Try now, in your imagination, to put yourself in that situation. Close your

eyes for a minute and really visualise yourself there. Have a good look around your imaginary world, your very own space that you have created.

5. Now come back to the situation in reality. Be aware of the things around you and where you are.

6. Practise shifting backwards and forwards into fantasy and back into reality.

7. Now be very aware of the situation you are in. The real world. With your eyes open, imagine you are bringing your fantasy space into the real world. Imagine you are putting it on, like a suit of clothes. Perhaps you can imagine yourself enclosed in a bubble which contains that peaceful situation.

8. Practise putting it on, and taking it off. All you have to do is think about that situation. See yourself in it.

9. Whenever you feel under some stress, in a tight situation and perhaps feeling a sense of craving for a cigarette, create a space around you which contains all the details you have built up in your fantasy.

Normally, when you are under stress, relaxing is the very last thing you can do. However, by creating a space, you can consciously change the direction of your mental functioning. Your perception of the situation can become more objective. You allow your mind to stay in its non-smoking groove. Your mental functioning can remain more stable and calm and you won't trigger negative emotional responses that may put you in danger of being pushed out of your track. Remember, as soon as you feel that you are spiralling downwards into an emotionally tense state, create a space.

It is probably not part of your normal behaviour to suddenly stop what you are doing, and to close your eyes for a few moments. However, if you make yourself do it when you feel tense or if you feel like smoking a cigarette, you will keep yourself cool and calm, and in control of yourself.

Exercise

Taking a brisk walk or going for a short run is beneficial for your health and many people find moderate exercise to be an excellent way of relieving tension and reducing the desire to smoke. Combine some exercise or activity with the other techniques you are already using. You will discover that you will begin to feel so much healthier.

Breathing away the desire to smoke

Deep breathing, combined with another awareness-heightening technique, taking your pulse, will relax you and move your awareness away from the desire to smoke to concern about your health. Use this technique when the desire to smoke is very intense. Do not, however, use this technique in place of deprogramming. This technique should be reserved for near-crisis situations.

- Empty your lungs as completely as you can – this requires some effort. Now breathe in deeply and slowly.

- Hold your breath for a moment.
- Finally, breathe out fast. If possible, breathe out explosively, relaxing yourself fully.
- Now take your pulse. Your radial pulse point is on the inside of your wrist, just below the base of your thumb. Press your fingertips lightly to the pulse point, watch the second hand of a clock or watch, count the beats over the course of fifteen seconds and multiply the result by four. Record your pulse rate. This will remind you of how healthy you are becoming as an ex-smoker.
- You should carry on breathing deeply while taking your pulse.
- Repeat the procedure, if necessary, then become occupied with something interesting. Involve yourself fully with that activity, as if it were the most important thing in the world.

Encouraging words

We all respond well to encouragement. In this book you will find some encouraging thoughts, should you find yourself having to fight any battles. Remember, giving encouragement to others is also very strengthening. If you know someone else who is quitting smoking, phone them and encourage them to keep up the good work. Or phone a friend for a chat – they'll probably be pleased to hear from you.

It is also important to encourage yourself! There is a very simple, but useful technique which will help you stop generating negative thoughts. Your mind may generate thoughts such as: I'm no good, I'm a failure. I'll never do it. The others will stop, but I'll fail for sure. I can't do it. I'm weak. I've never been able to succeed. I'm hopeless. When you become aware of the fact that your Biocomputer is generating these thoughts and flooding your mind with them, mentally shout the word, 'Stop!' Then deliberately start generating positive encouraging thoughts. You may like to use a Positive Programming Card. Write down some positive, encouraging statements on a card and keep the card with you. If you feel that you are becoming discouraged, take out your card and read it through. Here are some good examples:

- Each and every day I am getting better and better.
- I am losing the desire to smoke.
- I am a successful non-smoker.
- I am becoming healthy, free and in control.

If your Biocomputer then starts telling you again, 'But I really am weak,' repeat 'Stop!' and go back to the positive programming.

Remember, whether you feel weak or strong, a success or a failure depends partly on what you tell yourself. Failures are often failures purely because they allow their Biocomputers to generate negative failure-oriented thoughts. With such thoughts flooding their minds, how can they be anything other than failures? By consciously and deliberately repeating positive thoughts and statements and passing them through your mind, your whole behaviour and attitude of mind will follow a much more positive and constructive direction. If you have a partner or friend who can also encourage you, so much the better. Ask them to encourage you as often as possible.

Distraction

If you are able to distract your mind from thinking about cigarettes for sixty seconds, your desire to smoke will pass the crisis point. To use a distraction technique, you simply focus on some problem that will keep your mind occupied for a short while. It may be necessary to really force yourself to get started but you will find that your mind becomes increasingly involved and the dominating desire to smoke will fade. If you enjoy crosswords, have some handy. If you feel like smoking, take out a crossword and work on it for a few minutes. Keep a book of short stories or a novel handy. If you feel like a smoke, read a few pages. Select a book that you know will hold your interest.

Willpower

Many smokers have asked me this question: should willpower be used on Stop-Day? The answer is a resounding 'Yes'. By now, you should find that you have enough self-belief, confidence and motivation to go full steam ahead, whatever happens, without smoking. If you have followed the procedures outlined, you should be able to manage this final stage by resisting any desire to smoke. You can make it! You will make it! Failure is not an option. No matter how bad things may get, you can make it. Just like the man on the sinking *Titanic* . . .

James's progress

On Saturday, James smoked five cigarettes. On Sunday, he did not feel like going out and only smoked two cigarettes. He was feeling pleased with himself. He planned setting a 'Stop-Day'. He used more of the visualisation and implementation intentions techniques. James decided to make Tuesday his Stop-Day. He woke up on Tuesday, ready for the challenge not to smoke. He felt like a cigarette in the afternoon but resisted. He did not smoke from Sunday to Thursday. He found Thursday evening difficult but he used 'create a space' and went for a brisk walk and then called into the pub for a drink with his friends. He refused to smoke. That was a major turning point. James resolved *never* to smoke again and he never has!

Summary

- Keep active, relaxed and reprogram constantly.
- Explore all of the different relaxation exercises at the weekend. Discover which ones work best for you and use them regularly from now on.
- Construct your very own Positive Programming Card. Use it every time you feel you need some

encouragement. Your partner or friends should also be enlisted to support and encourage you.

- On Stop-Day itself, a little bit of willpower may be necessary. But by then you will have made excellent progress and you should be able to succeed.

- When you have completed your Stop-Day without smoking, you are half-way to becoming a non-smoker.

PART THREE

LIVING AS A NON-SMOKER

Please note: Part Three is for the ex-smoker, a person who has successfully completed their Stop-Day. You need to have reduced your consumption to zero, and completed your Stop-Day without a single puff of a cigarette. If you have not done that, please return to the beginning of Part Two and set yourself an achievable Stop-Day. As soon as you have successfully completed your Stop-Day, then return here.

Part Three gives you all that you need to know about preventing lapses and relapses (Chapter 9), managing your weight (Chapter 10), becoming more active (Chapter 11) and acquiring life skills as an ex-smoker (Chapter 12).

The appendices provide additional resources for *Stop Smoking Now*.

9

Preventing lapses
and relapses

Congratulations! You have completed Part Two of *Stop Smoking Now*. You are regaining your life without nicotine. You are in the process of giving yourself a mega-boost of health, vitality and quality of life. You are on the way to becoming a brighter, calmer, cleaner, clearer, fresher, sharper, all-round healthier person. Your self-esteem will become stronger and your confidence will grow. Your non-smoking family members, friends, and colleagues will be breathing a huge sigh of relief. No longer will they be putting up with your addiction to tobacco. In short, you are becoming a new person, the person you want to be. You are on the road to recovery.

What next?

You are perfectly aware that all of the positive things you have achieved can go up in smoke if you are not careful to monitor your experience and behaviour. Use mindfulness. Use meditation. Be on your guard. You could still be very vulnerable to smoking triggers.

You have already reprogrammed your Biocomputer. You no longer enjoy smoking. It is no longer a pleasant experience. However, you will perhaps experience an emptiness. You have a lot of extra time on your hands. Your inner Chimp and Chameleon may both be feeling restless. You were previously spending perhaps the equivalent of one whole month or more out of every year smoking. A terrible waste of valuable time and money. For no benefits in return, only risking your health.

You may now be feeling a sense of anti-climax. Your restless mind, your Chimp brain, may continue to be restless. Your daily cycles of waking and sleeping, controlled by your Chameleon brain, may be disrupted. Some of your routines may be thrown slightly into turmoil. Triggers will appear as usual but nowadays you should not feel any strong compulsion to respond.

Deprogramming, reprogramming, eliminating triggers, reducing the desire to smoke, reducing your cigarette consumption and stopping smoking for one entire day are all important steps in overcoming your smoking habit. For most smokers who quit, it's relatively easy to stop smoking for the first few days. However, they often start smoking again. You need to be absolutely committed to making the change permanent.

Smokers are often left to their own devices just after they stop smoking and are given very little help. Yet this is the crucial stage where some informed guidance can make all of the difference. Quitting your smoking habit has involved many different processes: new skills, de- and reprogramming, relaxing, de-stressing and creating a different self-image. At this stage, you need strategies for maintaining a smoke-free lifestyle for the rest of your life. You will need to use coping strategies when you're with other smokers, especially when they're your work colleagues, friends, or family members.

Here in Part Three we deal with strategies for making your freedom from nicotine permanent. Part Three will help you to:

- Learn how to prevent lapses and relapses.
- Be fully aware of the psychological factors that come into play when you have not smoked for an interval of time that is increasing.
- Learn new coping skills to help you deal with problems that may appear.
- Learn how to keep a check on your weight.
- Look at how you can increase your physical activity.
- Learn how to set up a new balance in your life in which smoking no longer plays a role.

A life that flows smoothly is joyful – the diamond stylus

The situation of the ex-smoker is precarious. Two psychologists, Alan Marlatt and Judith Gordon, suggested that the smoker's life is a bit like a vinyl record spinning on the turntable. A diamond needle creates music by moving along the spiral groove to produce sound from the record. The music on the record flows from beginning to end, like a smoker's life flows from the past to the present, and into the future. We live only in the present. We hear now only the music that is playing at this very moment. For enjoyable music, we need a smooth, continuous movement of the needle, without any disruption. Occasionally, however, a piece of dirt or dust sits in the groove, causing the needle to jump. This jump spoils the music and causes a disruption to the flow. When the diamond stylus of your life jumps into the wrong groove, you risk lapsing into the smoking habits of your past. You have to put the needle back where it belongs, in the right place on the track and this isn't easy to find.

The diamond stylus. Like music from a record player, a life that flows smoothly is joyful. A jumping stylus is disruptive and causes chaos (photograph reproduced courtesy of a creative commons licence from Moehre 1992, Wikipedia).

When a smoking lapse occurs and the stylus has jumped back into the wrong groove, you are abruptly taken to a previous stage of the record, repeating everything that has gone before, as if you never managed to give up smoking.

When it happens, you fear that it's going to repeat itself again and again. Just as there are many forces that can make a needle jump out of its groove (e.g. dust, grease, scratches, cracks and breaks), so there are many factors that could knock you out of your non-smoking groove unless you are very careful – such as unexpected events, accidents, blows, bad luck and arguments, or when the stresses and strains of everyday living become intolerable.

Consider the following situation. Sandra has not smoked for four days, since the previous Monday. Today is Friday, always a rush and she has had a tough day at the office and has been working under a lot of pressure. This has led to a disagreement with her boss and her colleagues. Sandra comes home to find an unexpectedly high electricity bill waiting. She decides to use her credit card – until she checks the balance and discovers she's borrowed up to the limit. Sandra cooks dinner with her partner, Sam, and they share a bottle of wine. They relax after dinner in front of the TV. Sam lights a cigarette (unhelpful!). Sandra experiences a compelling, forceful desire to smoke. After fighting it for a few minutes, she finally gives in and decides to have a cigarette.

This backslides Sandra right out of her non-smoking groove into her old groove as a smoker. Now she is faced with the task of quitting smoking all over again. It is easy to pinpoint a few of the forces that pulled Sandra so abruptly out of her groove:

- Stress during Sandra's day at work.
- Sandra's physical addiction to nicotine.

- Sandra's reprogramming not yet complete.
- Alcohol acting as a trigger.
- Sam's smoking acting as a trigger.
- How many others?

Using CBT is giving you many advantages over someone as unprepared as Sandra. You have put into place psychological methods for removing your smoking programs and this type of lapse is therefore much less likely to occur.

However, there is still a danger that triggers that have not yet been permanently reprogrammed will crop up. Some of these may not have occurred during your last seven to ten days as a smoker and therefore you will not have had a proper opportunity to reprogram them. You may also be suffering from the last stages of nicotine addiction that might give you withdrawal symptoms and put you at risk of smoking again. There are solutions to these problems, but it will take more effort on your part. The next section gives further details about what you can do.

The benefits of quitting

It is useful now to assess what the benefits of stopping really are. Consider them in turn and then compile a full list of your own.

Rediscovered senses

You may have noticed already how your senses of taste and smell have livened up. Many ex-smokers can't believe how tasty food really is and how many scents they were unable to smell when they were smokers. You may find your appetite changes slightly and foods or drinks that previously seemed bland become quite delicious. Some smokers worry that their new enthusiasm for eating will result in weight gain. A few pounds certainly may go on after stopping smoking, but you can just as easily take them off again or at least limit the increase, by following the guidelines in Chapters 10 and 11.

Cleanliness

You may notice the stench of stale smoke on your clothes. The smell of your hair and breath will improve greatly when you stop smoking. You may dislike the smell of smoke and start to avoid social situations where smoking occurs. You will certainly feel fresher, brighter, and cleaner.

Physical health and fitness

Your health will improve as soon as you stop inhaling nicotine and carbon monoxide. These health improvements kick in at different times; the box on the following page gives more details. You may feel a lot more active and you will be able to exercise for longer periods before you become tired. You could increase your level of physical activity by walking more, or taking more vigorous exercise such as running. If you are thinking of starting a more vigorous programme of exercise, it would be wise to consult your doctor first, to check the state of your heart and cardiovascular system. Follow the guidelines in Chapter 11.

Not everyone will experience all the changes listed in the box, especially people who lead sedentary lives or those who are already physically active. But the long-term benefits of stopping smoking are considerable. Within a few years, your level of risk for smoking-related critical illnesses will fall to near-normal levels. Studies have found that the risk of lung cancer is reduced by 50 per cent in just five years after stopping smoking. Other evidence suggests that this reduction in risk kicks in even earlier.

Health improvements after quitting smoking

Within 20 minutes of your last cigarette:
- You stop polluting the air.
- Blood pressure drops to normal.
- Pulse rate drops to normal rate.
- Temperature of hands and feet increases to normal.

8 hours:
- Carbon monoxide level in blood drops to normal.
- Oxygen level in blood increases to normal.

24 hours:
- Chance of heart attack decreases.

48 hours:
- Nerve endings adjust to the absence of nicotine.
- Ability to smell and taste things is enhanced.

---

72 hours:
- Bronchial tubes relax, making breathing easier.
- Lung capacity increases.

Two weeks to three months:
- Circulation improves.
- Walking becomes easier.
- Lung function increases up to 30 per cent.

One to nine months:
- Coughing, sinus congestion, fatigue and shortness of breath all decrease.
- Cilia (hair-like projections) regrow in lungs, increasing the ability of the lungs to handle mucus, clean the lungs and reduce infection.
- Body's overall energy level increases.

One year:
- Rate of death from heart disease is halfway back to that of a non-smoker.

Five years:
- Rate of death from disease is the same as that of a non-smoker.

Ten years:
- Rate of death from lung cancer drops almost to the rate of a non-smoker.
- Precancerous cells are replaced. The incidence of other cancers (such as mouth, larynx, oesophagus, bladder, kidney, and pancreas) decreases.

Women's health

Research shows that women benefit even more than men from quitting smoking. Findings from the Lung Health Study in the USA indicate that women's lung function improves significantly more than men's after sustained smoking cessation. All participants had mild or moderate chronic obstructive pulmonary disease (COPD). In the first year after quitting smoking, the women's lung function improved more than twice that of the men's, although the difference between the genders narrowed over time.

Studies indicate that menopause occurs between 0.8 and 1.7 years earlier in smokers than in non-smokers. Smoking can cause reduced fertility in women; in one study, smokers were more than three times more likely than non-smokers to have taken more than a year to conceive a child. It was estimated that women who smoked were only 72 per cent as fertile as non-smokers. Smoking can also cause miscarriage. The Royal College of Physicians has suggested that there are four thousand miscarriages a year in the UK caused by smoking.

Smoking during pregnancy carries significant risks for both mother and baby. The mother's airways function less well and may leave her physically unready for the birth process. The birth weight of the baby is also likely to be lighter and, as the baby grows, it is likely to remain shorter and lighter. This is because nicotine constricts the blood vessels, including the ones to the placenta and the baby, so the baby does not get enough oxygen and nutrients. However, the baby's health would be fine if the mother were to quit smoking about a month before trying to conceive. As already discussed in Chapter 1, an expectant mother should have no nicotine at all in her system during pregnancy.

Sex

Many ex-smokers report that their interest in sex – and their actual sexual performance – increases after they quit smoking. This could be for several reasons. Firstly, they feel more virile, attractive and more sexy. Ready, willing and able! Secondly, the drug nicotine has a dulling effect on sexual appetite. Thirdly, the ex-smoker is more capable physically, runs out of breath less easily and should be more sensitive to their partner's needs.

Several recent studies have looked at how smoking affects male impotence and found that there is a link between smoking and difficulties having an erection. Men who smoke are more likely to experience impotence and loss of stamina. Overall, smoking increases the risk of impotence by about 50 per cent for men in their thirties and forties. But the link between smoking and male impotence affects women as well. Nicotine is a vasoconstrictor, tightening blood vessels and restricting blood flow. In the long term, it causes permanent damage to arteries.

Since a man's erection depends on blood flow, it seems likely that smoking would affect erections. Studies have confirmed this. Forty per cent of men affected by impotence are smokers, as opposed to 28 per cent of the general male population.

If you are a man, it's difficult to say whether your sex life will definitely improve now that you have stopped smoking, since many factors influence your sex life in addition to your ability to have an erection, but it certainly can help. Quitting smoking eliminates stained teeth, unhealthy skin, the rapid accumulation of wrinkles on the face and the stink of smoke on your clothing, hair and breath – and this will make you more attractive to your partner.

Money

If health, fitness, and sex aren't enough to give you satisfaction, perhaps money will! A smoker burns through piles of money on cigarettes and this is money that they can usually ill-afford. You may be surprised to work out exactly how much you spend each year as a smoker. These figures will help with the calculation.

1. Within two to five years, your risk of stroke is substantially reduced. You've also saved between £7,000 and £17,000.
2. After ten to fourteen years, your risk of dying from cancer is nearly the same as that of a lifetime non-smoker. You've also saved over thirty-five thousand pounds.
3. After fifteen years, your risk of coronary heart disease is nearly the same as that of a lifetime non-smoker. You've also saved over fifty thousand pounds.
4. At today's prices, if you smoke one pack of cigarettes

per day for ten years, you'll spend over thirty-five thousand pounds – easily enough to buy a new luxury car.

Take time again now to calculate how much you're used to spending per week on cigarettes. For every pound a week spent on cigarettes during a working lifetime from the ages of twenty to sixty-five, your cash outlay would be £2,340. If you invested this pound a week at 5 per cent, the real cost would be £8,719. If you spend £65.80 a week on cigarettes, this figure would be **£573,710**. If your partner also smokes, that makes a total of more than one million pounds gone up in smoke. You could be healthy and fit non-smoking millionaires. Do you really want to trade that in for cancer and heart disease?

Parents

One of the greatest benefits to parents who quit smoking must be the example that they set to their children. Your children are more likely to smoke if you are a smoker. A Seattle, USA, study published in 2000 showed that parents who quit smoking before their child reached third grade (usually at the age of around eight to nine) significantly reduced their child's chances of becoming a smoker by the time of their senior year of high school (when children are generally aged around seventeen or eighteen). If one parent quit smoking by the time the child was eight or nine years old, the child's chances of being a daily or monthly smoker at age seventeen or eighteen decreased by 25 per cent. If both parents quit, the child's chances of smoking dropped by nearly 40 per cent. If all smoking parents were to quit by the time their children were around age eight, this might be able to prevent 136,000 young people in the USA from becoming daily, long-term smokers, the researchers concluded.

It is likely that the same trends would be seen elsewhere. We act as role models for our children. If they see us smoking, how can we expect them not to be tempted?

Self-esteem

Other major benefits will be to your mental health, your sense of well-being, and your self-esteem. It is very difficult to feel good about yourself when you are trapped in a habit over which you have so little control. By ridding yourself of the habit, you will feel freer, more in control of yourself, and have higher self-esteem. This factor is often overlooked, but for many it is this increased sense of personal freedom, and all that this means, which makes stopping smoking worthwhile.

The World Health Organisation has reported on the links between self-esteem, self-image and tobacco use. Adolescents who smoke tend to have low self-esteem and low expectations for future achievement. They see smoking as a way to cope with the feelings of stress, anxiety and depression that stem from a lack of self-confidence. Any smoker who quits receives a helpful boost in self-esteem.

Personal list of benefits gained from stopping smoking permanently

After considering the benefits listed above, give some thought to your own position. Write a list of your own personal benefits in the following table.

1 ————————————————————————

2 ————————————————————————

3 ————————————————————————

4 ————————————————————————

5 ————————————————————————

6 ————————————————————————

7 ————————————————————————

8 ————————————————————————

9 ————————————————————————

10 ————————————————————————

Think about these benefits and enjoy them. Mentally rehearse all of the desired outcomes of your new life as a permanent non-smoker.

Other methods to help you stop smoking

Health authorities claim that using forms of nicotine replacement therapy (NRT) such as patches or gum increases your chances of success. However, not everybody agrees. John R. Polito of whyquit.com claims that patches do not produce results any better than quitting on your own and do far worse than intensive programmes such as CBT.

I reviewed the evidence on NRT in Chapter 2. I have to admit to having mixed feelings about including this section and was on the point of deleting it. However, in the spirit of 'give anything a try if you're desperate' I have left it. My personal estimate of whether NRT will actually help you is 50:50. By this I mean that I would give you a 50 per cent chance of being helped by NRT. How much it will help you, should you decide to use it, is debatable. It might just get you through a bad patch (sorry, no pun intended) but I would not rely on it. In my opinion, it's a method for losers. By that I mean it's a method for people who have failed to stop smoking using the powers of their mind. To rely on it would be pure folly. You could end up addicted to nicotine for the rest of your life and, in all probability, return to smoking and be using gum or patches. That would be simply the worst of both worlds.

With reservations, warnings and provisos, I am suggesting that for around 5–10 per cent of ex-smokers who have used CBT to stop smoking, NRT might be helpful when used for a limited period of time. How helpful it can be, however, is a complete unknown as there are no clinical trials in which NRT has been compared to a placebo after a course of CBT.

Given the lack of empirical evidence, one can only rely on past experience. I know that there are a few cases in which NRT did help people get over the hump of nicotine withdrawal for a short period of time. However, the vast majority (90 per cent) of ex-smokers who used CBT did not need to use NRT. Ideally, you will not need to use NRT at all. I strongly recommend that you do not use NRT for longer than three to four weeks. To use NRT for more than three weeks implies that you are still addicted to nicotine.

This means that you still have Biocomputer programs that have not been properly extinguished. Further deprogramming is needed. In such cases, NRT can help to reduce withdrawal symptoms.

There are six main nicotine replacement products that you can consider:

1. Nicotine gum
2. Nicotine patches
3. Nicotine inhaler
4. Nicotine nasal spray
5. Sublingual tablets
6. Lozenges

These products vary according to speed of absorption, ease of use, frequency of use, type of side effects, and potential for the user to vary the dose to suit the needs of the moment.

Nicotine gum

Nicotine chewing gum is available from your local pharmacist without a prescription. Taken sensibly and in moderation, it can be a useful aid at this stage. Although everything that can possibly be done to minimise withdrawal symptoms has been included in this programme (for example, meditation, relaxation and gradual reduction), it is still possible to experience withdrawal symptoms if your consumption was high or you had been a smoker for a very long time.

If you use nicotine products, it is essential to follow the manufacturer's directions. The gum should be used only when you feel the need for it during the first ten to thirty following your Stop-Day. This will take the edge off any bad feelings that may result from stopping smoking.

Manufacturers recommend that you keep the gum in your cheek. You will then have it ready to chew on whenever you need it. Chew the gum only until you notice a slight tingling or peppery taste from the nicotine being released. Then keep the gum between your cheek and gum, so the nicotine can be absorbed. You should chew every four to five minutes for thirty minutes, until all the nicotine is released. You can use up to thirty pieces a day. Hopefully your own usage will not need to be this high because you have already done a lot of deprogramming using the CBT.

Nicotine gum comes in packs of different sizes. You may require relatively few number of pieces because your deprogramming and reprogramming will have achieved a lot in breaking your addiction to nicotine. Many CBT ex-smokers manage perfectly well with no gum at all.

Do not drink any hot liquids, tea or coffee, while the gum is in your mouth. Remove the gum, drink your beverage and then re-insert the gum.

Always use the gum under medical supervision, especially if you have heart disease or are pregnant. Keep gum away from children and pets.

Different flavours are available, including spearmint, to disguise the bitter taste of nicotine and make the gum more palatable. A small minority of smokers have completely replaced the nicotine they obtained from smoking by chewing the gum! However, this is not very likely in your case, if you have already reduced your cigarette consumption to zero using this programme. The gum should be used as a very temporary bridge between smoking and non-smoking. It could therefore make some difference in the first one to four weeks after stopping.

Some ex-smokers resist the idea of using the gum because they feel that they are replacing one kind of dependency with another. There are also possible side effects from the gum: sore jaw, mouth irritation, nausea, sore throat, heartburn, and rapid heartbeat. On the other hand, it is better to use the gum for a few weeks than to give in to the desire to smoke and lose everything that you have achieved so far. After a few weeks you will find that you can easily manage without the gum and you will then be free of nicotine forever.

Nicotine patches

Another way of replacing nicotine is to use nicotine patches. These provide nicotine transdermally (through the skin) and have similar properties to nicotine gum, with the added advantage that the user can avoid the unpleasant taste. The patches help to abolish withdrawal symptoms, including irritability, tiredness and the craving. Patches supply a constant amount of nicotine in the bloodstream for the time the patch is attached, which should help to overcome the worst of the physical withdrawal effects, but they will not give the same effect or 'kick' as inhaling on your cigarette.

There are different strengths of patches. The dosages are designed for smokers who are using patches and nothing else so please be very careful not to overdose yourself. Heavy smokers normally start on the highest strength and work down. Because you have been using CBT, you can probably skip the higher dose and start off with a moderate dosage, gradually reducing this.

There are a large number of possible side effects. The patches definitely should *not* be used during pregnancy and breast-feeding or by those who suffer from heart problems, stroke or diseases of the skin. Please discuss the use of these with your doctor or pharmacist before starting to use them. Nicotine patches are available over the counter and, in the UK, they are also available from the NHS. Their prescription is linked to counselling in a local smoking cessation clinic. Please be careful with your patches and keep them locked away from the hands of infants, children, teenagers and pregnant women who may be unaware of the dangers.

Nicotine inhaler

The nicotine level from an inhaler peaks in twenty to thirty minutes. You can use the inhaler for up to twenty minutes every hour. About ten puffs on the inhalator is equivalent to one puff of a cigarette. It may cause coughing and throat irritation.

Nicotine nasal spray

This product has the highest potential to recreate your dependence on nicotine so, in general, I do not recommend it. This product gives the most rapid relief from cravings. You can give one squirt to each nostril, once or twice per hour. It can be quite unpleasant at first, irritating your nose and throat and it can make your nose runny.

Sublingual tablets

The 2 mg tablets dissolve under the tongue in twenty minutes, when the nicotine level peaks. Quitters normally have up to thirty tablets a day to replace cigarettes. However, your requirements, following CBT, should be much lower than this. The side effects are a stinging mouth, hiccups, and some gastric effects.

Lozenges

These come in 1, 2, or 4 mg doses and dissolve in the mouth in about twenty minutes. You move them around with your tongue every few seconds. As with sublingual tablets, the side effects are a stinging mouth, hiccups and gastric symptoms.

Social skills for the ex-smoker

The new, non-smoking-you will need skills and strategies to deal with the traps and pitfalls set by anybody who envies or resents the fact you no longer smoke, because they are still a smoker. This is one of the factors determining your long-term success or failure. Social pressure from smokers can sabotage your best efforts to quit. Fortunately, you have a rich store of information about smoker psychology because, until very recently, you were one.

A useful analogy is to think what it is like when, as a sober person, you deal with a person who is drunk: a fair degree of patience is needed because you are dealing with a person who cannot think logically or clearly and whose befuddled mind is confused by splits in consciousness. You need to listen to what they say, but at the same time treat some of what is said with a large pinch of salt. In a friendly but firm manner, you will need to assert your right to choose not to smoke. Smokers will learn to accept this and respect you for making this decision. In fact, these days, there is such a stigma attached to smoking that the pushy smoker is a fairly rare phenomenon.

Depending upon circumstances and how many smokers there are among your family, friends, and acquaintances, you will be exposed to a variety of opportunities to smoke.

You must never accept a cigarette when it is offered, nor weaken and ask for one. You will need to practise being assertive while in the company of addicted smokers.

Many recent ex-smokers are struck by the selfishness of smokers. This experience can be somewhat shaming as you realise how you yourself must have invaded other people's right to breathe clean, smokeless air over the period when you were a smoker. Therefore, one of the biggest dangers for the new ex-smoker is to become rampantly anti-smoking. A tolerant, patient attitude is the best approach in the early days of non-smoking, no matter how secretly triumphant you feel on the inside.

The ex-smoker who quickly converts to being strongly anti-smoking probably still carries active Pro-Cigarette

Programs (PCPs) and is therefore still at risk. Deep down, some of the oldest, most stubborn PCPs are still partially active. Newer, non-smoking programs eventually override most PCPs. However, the fear that their deprogramming remains incomplete often motivates the most fervent anti-smoking evangelists. If you find yourself protesting to an extreme degree about other people smoking, you need to remain on your guard. You probably have some deprogramming to do. Archaic triggers could remain partially hidden under cover of your consciousness. You must practise mental rehearsal at regular intervals to expel them. Choose the triggers that worry you the most and imagine yourself coping with them, even under severe provocation from others. By vividly imagining yourself happily dealing with these triggers, you will be able to supplant your PCPs with newer, more adaptive action programs. See yourself interacting with others and smokers in particular, in ways that will minimise stress and conflict.

Continue to use relaxation in its various forms: meditating, fantasy, creating a space and the other procedures described in Part 2. Continue to make time for these activities as a rite of passage.

Activity

You will find that you have more time on your hands as a result of stopping smoking. Many previous cigarette moments appear as gaps to be filled. Relaxation and other new activities are excellent ways of filling the vacuum.

Many people say that they do not know what to do with their hands when they give up smoking. That is unsurprising, when you think how much manual and oral activity goes into the behaviour of the regular smoker. You probably took 200 to 400 puffs of tobacco every day of your smoking life. There is the ritual of:

1. taking out your cigarettes
2. playing with one in your fingers
3. lighting a match or lighter
4. igniting the cigarette
5. taking the first puff
6. etc.

You were perhaps addicted to the ritual as much as to the nicotine; away from the act of smoking itself, many smokers also fiddle with their cigarettes or lighter while doing other things. Some ex-smokers find it helpful to play with a stress ball, a bunch of keys, or to doodle. Take up knitting, crosswords, or jigsaw puzzles – anything to keep your fingers busy for a few minutes until the desire to smoke passes. Some people take a sip of water or fruit juice every time they feel like smoking a cigarette. Doing a few push-ups or going for a run around the block can also help to relieve tension and keep your mind and body occupied when the desire for a cigarette becomes difficult to push away. The main thing is to keep your Biocomputer busy with interesting things while mentally vacuuming, so that dormant PCPs can't keep popping out. There's nothing they like better than a passive, empty mind to fill! By now they should be seriously weakened, but if your mind is inactive something has to fill the vacuum.

Another option is to take up a few more physical activities. Full details about using physical activity for health and leisure can be found in Chapter 11.

The fail-safe procedure

Now for the 'crunch' questions: what happens if everything suddenly fails? What will you do if, for some reason, you feel that you really *have* to smoke? What insurance policy do you have against that moment when you simply cannot resist smoking?

These are the questions that worry most ex-smokers, especially during the first few days after Stop-Day. They do have answers. There is an insurance policy. There is a failsafe procedure. Although it is incredibly simple, it is one of the most crucial procedures in this entire programme. Use it if you ever feel that you cannot possibly avoid having a cigarette. Unfortunately, it is not very pleasant. However, it is far better to experience a few unpleasant minutes than to start smoking again, which will be what happens if you let yourself play the Just One Game. The fail-safe procedure is also called the 'Smoke Two Rule'. This is what you should do. Light a cigarette and smoke it. Then light a second cigarette and smoke and smoke, until you feel so sick that you cannot smoke any more. You may need a third cigarette to really get smoking out of your system.

However, if you do smoke until you are almost sick, you will not be at risk of developing the habit ever again. Experience with lapsing non-smokers has shown that the fail-safe procedure is a successful prevention device. Use it, should you ever need to do so, at any time in the future. Your ability to remain a non-smoker forever is then a strong possibility.

Summary

- Make a list of the benefits that you personally will obtain from making non-smoking permanent.
- Learn social skills for dealing with smokers: be assertive, tolerant, and patient.
- Continue to use methods of relaxation.
- Keep your mind active – an empty mind is vulnerable to dormant PCPs that may spring back to life again if there is nothing to distract it.
- If all else fails, use the fail-safe procedure.
- Enjoy your first few weeks as an ex-smoker!

10

Managing your weight

One of the biggest fears about quitting smoking is the danger of putting on weight. You may have gained a pound or two already and you could be concerned about your waistline and looks. If so, do not despair. By using the tools and techniques explained in this chapter, you can limit the extra weight you put on, and avoid any increases larger than is absolutely necessary.

It is important that you know that the health benefits of stopping smoking far exceed any health risks that may result from smoking cessation-induced body weight gain. Left unattended, it is unlikely that your weight gain would exceed 4–5 kg one year after stopping. However, do not despair; there are effective methods for preventing weight gain described in this and the following chapter.

There are hundreds of weight control and dieting systems available. Unfortunately, the majority make bogus claims that can never be substantiated with any evidence. They appeal to the panic and desperation that can overtake a person who sees their weight escalating and feels like they are running out of control.

One day, I received the following spam email:

> Hello, I have a special offer for you . . . WANT TO LOSE WEIGHT?
>
> The most powerful weight loss is now available without prescription . . .
>
> *100 per cent money-back guarantee!*
>
> * *Lose up to 19 per cent total bodyweight.*
>
> * *Up to 300 per cent more weight loss while dieting.*
>
> * *Loss of 20–35 per cent abdominal fat.*
>
> * *Reduction of 40–70 per cent overall fat under skin.*
>
> * *Increase metabolic rate by 76.9 per cent without exercise.*
>
> * *Boost your confidence level and self-esteem.*

There are several features of this message that are difficult to believe. The figures seem spuriously precise – e.g. why 76.9 per cent and not 77 per cent (in keeping with the other percentages)? We cannot be sure whether such offers are going to be helpful to the recent quitter, but they really do sound highly implausible. If no evidence is offered that a particular product would help you in this situation, then it's likely that no evidence exists. Rather than relying on magical cures in the form of herbs, pills and potions, a much surer approach is to take the problem into your own hands by controlling your eating behaviour yourself and increasing your levels of activity. The basic equation is as follows:

Energy stored as fat (Fat) = energy in (Food) − energy out (Exercise)

Or, put more simply,

FAT = FOOD MINUS EXERCISE

You can immediately see what you need to do if you want to take off any increased weight. Eat less fatty foods and take more exercise.

Another worry for some people is that they will drink more alcohol when they give up smoking and risk becoming an alcoholic. One ex-smoker told me that he'd never had any real problems giving up smoking, although he confessed that alcohol 'helped'. I asked him how much he was drinking and he told me about a half-bottle of whisky every evening! However, substituting alcohol for smoking is not all that common and the evidence suggests that smokers drink more than ex-smokers. This is a less common worry, but some ex-smokers definitely feel the need for something to replace their puffing on cigarettes.

Making some small but persistent adjustments to your eating or drinking habits and to your present level of physical activity is usually all that is required. You will find many different approaches to try here, and you should select methods that have the most appeal to you personally. As you work through this chapter, have a pencil handy so that you can write down your answers to the questions, and tick the relevant boxes when you come to a technique that you would like to try. Developing your new life as a non-smoker will take some time, as you will have many small adjustments to make. Gradual but successful improvements are what you should be aiming for, rather than radical, instantaneous solutions.

This chapter concentrates on eating because that is what usually causes most concern, but everything suggested can be applied equally well to drinking habits.

Are you a healthy weight?

Take a straight line across from your height (without shoes) and a line up from your weight (without clothes). Put a mark where the two lines meet.

UNDERWEIGHT: Maybe you need to eat a bit more. But go for well-balanced nutritious foods and don't just fill up on fatty and sugary foods. If you are very underweight, see your doctor about it.

OK: You're eating the right quantity of food but you need to be sure that you're getting a healthy balance in your diet.

OVERWEIGHT: You should try to lose weight.

OBESE: You need to lose weight.

MORBIDLY OBESE: You urgently need to lose weight.

You would do well to see your doctor, who might refer you to a nutritionist.

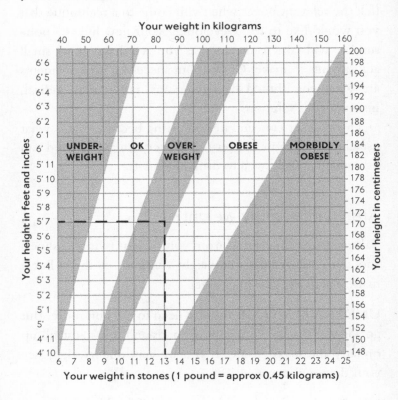

A Few Key Questions

A good way of beginning to think about your eating habits is to answer the five questions below. Place a mark in the column that best describes your current eating behaviour:

	Never	Some-times	Very often

1. Since stopping smoking, have you noticed yourself eating more at meal times? ☐ ☐ ☐

How much more? A second helping?

Any particular types of food? Please specify:

_____

_____

_____

2. Have you noticed yourself eating between meals more often than you did in the past? ☐ ☐ ☐

How much more often? What sorts of foods? Are these the same sorts of snacks or are they different from those you used to eat when you smoked?

_____

_____

_____

3. Have you noticed yourself eating when the past you have lit up a cigarette? ☐ ☐ ☐

At what sort of times? Please specify:

_____

_____

_____

4. Thinking back over the last week, have you found yourself doing the following

a) watching TV

b) reading

c) listening to the radio/music

d) sewing/knitting/writing

e) cooking

f) working

g) shopping

h) driving

Other situations? Please specify:

i) _____

j) _____

k) _____

5. Can you remember yourself eating in situations where you were feeling any of these emotions?

a) angry

b) worried

c) sad

d) lonely

e) tired

f) depressed

g) nervous

h) excited

Other feelings? Please specify:

i) _____

j) _____

k) _____

Mindfulness: eating one raisin

It is a good idea at this time to be mindful about your eating. Being mindful about eating will help you to become aware of 'being' rather than 'doing'. Think about who you are — are you being the real you or are you distracted from thinking about the real you by doing many things and eating many things that are part of a frantic lifestyle? This includes habits and conforming to trends, doing as other people do, squeezing out healthful eating in favour of stress-related eating, convenience foods, foods that are heavily processed, fast foods, ready meals and snacking on salty and fattening foods. Is this the you you want to be or the you that is a slave to conditioning and life-long habits that are serving you no worthwhile purpose?

Please try the following exercise. You will need a raisin or a nut from your kitchen.

Holding

First, take a raisin and hold it in the palm of your hand or between your finger and thumb. Focusing on it, imagine that you've just dropped in from Mars and have never seen an object like this before in your life.

Seeing

Take time to really see it; gaze at the raisin with care and full attention. Let your eyes explore every part of it, examining the highlights where the light shines, the darker hollows, the folds and ridges and any asymmetries or unique features.

Touching

Turn the raisin over between your fingers, exploring its texture, maybe with your eyes closed if that enhances your sense of touch.

Smelling

Holding the raisin beneath your nose, with each inhalation drink in any smell, aroma or fragrance that may arise, noticing as you do this anything interesting that may be happening in your mouth or stomach.

Placing

Now slowly bring the raisin up to your lips, noticing how your hand and arm know exactly how and where to position it. Gently place the object in the mouth, without chewing, noticing how it gets into the mouth in the first place. Spend a few moments exploring the sensations of having it in your mouth, exploring it with your tongue.

Tasting

When you are ready, prepare to chew the raisin, noticing how and where it needs to be for chewing. Then, very consciously, take one or two bites into it and notice what happens in the aftermath, experiencing any waves of taste that emanate from it as you continue chewing. Without swallowing yet, notice the bare sensations of taste and texture in the mouth and how these may change over time, moment by moment, as well as any changes in the object itself.

Swallowing

When you feel ready to swallow the raisin, see if you can first detect the intention to swallow as it comes up, so that even this is experienced consciously before you actually swallow the raisin.

Following

Finally, see if you can feel what is left of the raisin moving down into your stomach, and sense how the body as a whole is feeling after completing this exercise in mindful eating.

This exercise is reproduced from: Mark Williams, John Teasdale, Zindel Segal, and Jon Kabat-Zinn (2007). *The Mindful Way through Depression: Freeing Yourself from Chronic Unhappiness*. New York: Guilford Press.

Constructing your personal eating CBT programme

Using the ideas below, please select three of the many possible ways in which you can control your weight and use them for the next three weeks. When you can see that you have made some real progress, you should try some of the other possibilities during the weeks that follow.

There are many possibilities presented here. As you answer each question, really try to give an honest answer. This will allow you to develop a personal programme that suits you. You will not be able to do all of these things at once but, as you read about each one, consider it as if you were going to do it. When you have finished reading all of them, you will be able to choose the specific changes you would like to make and the methods you will use to make those changes. Think about each question carefully and then write the answers in the spaces provided.

1. Eating at Mealtimes

If you wanted to reduce the amount you eat at mealtimes by just a little, which specific food items can you imagine yourself leaving? If you choose fatty or sweet foods, then you will only have to reduce the amount you eat by just a little to eliminate a lot of calories. Write some of your initial ideas inside this box:

A

2. Eating between meals

If you wanted to control snacking, or eating between meals, what do you think would be easier or more convenient to control? Tick the appropriate box.

How often you eat between meals   B ☐

or

The amount of food that you eat on each occasion   C ☐

or

The fat content of your snacks   D ☐

3. Substituting eating for smoking

Have you noticed yourself eating at times when in the past you would have lit up a cigarette? If so, write down one or two of those kinds of situations that you would like to control.

E

F

4. Trigger Situations

In question four of the key questions above (page 250), did you tick any situations in the *Very Often* or *Sometimes* columns? If you did, which two would you most like to be able to control by not eating or over-eating? (If you ticked the *Never* column for all situations, please leave the two panels below blank).

G

H

5. Trigger Emotions

In question five, above, did you tick any of the emotions in the *Very Often* or *Sometimes* columns? Which two would you most like to be able to handle without needing to eat something?

I

When I am feeling . . .

J

When I am feeling . . .

---

6. Prioritise

Look at your answers, A–J, and see if you still agree with them. Having made any corrections or adjustments, decide which are the most important to work on. Tick the three most important ones. Of these three, which would be easiest to control? Which would be the most difficult to control? And which would be in between? Write the corresponding letter in each box below:

The easiest to control ❏

The second easiest to control ❏

The most difficult to control ❏

These three changes are the ones that you should concentrate on over the next three weeks. Start immediately with the easiest, the next easiest in three days' time and the most difficult in one week's time. Now that you have decided what your priorities are, study the next section to discover how to begin changing and modifying your eating behaviour.

The techniques

Try the techniques corresponding to the three priorities you have selected. The more you enjoy using the techniques, the more successful they will be. As you work through this section, you will need a pencil. When you come across an idea that appeals to you, place a mark in the box. Later you will be able to quickly select the best techniques to try.

1. Reducing the amount you eat at meal times

Having stopped smoking, you are able to prevent an increase in your weight by decreasing the quantity of food that you eat. This needs to be only a very small amount at each meal. The first thing you must *not* do is to try to force yourself to do things using willpower. When people focus on something they know they shouldn't really have, they end up wanting it all the more. There is a child in every adult, screaming to do everything it wants. If you constantly say to yourself things like, 'I'm on a diet. I'm depriving myself. That food looks really delicious,' it is very likely that you will build up a strong desire to eat more. Here is a set of guidelines that minimises the need for willpower.

1. Reduce the amount you eat by a small quantity at each meal. Don't deprive yourself of major quantities of enjoyable food by going on a crash diet, which never work – and you know it. How you think about what you are doing will affect how well you cope with it. Rather than thinking that you are depriving yourself, see yourself as confidently and surely developing your health by eating just a little less. ❑

2. Use a smaller plate so that your portion seems larger than it really is. This helps to prevent overeating by reducing the amount you eat by just a little without actually noticing it. Research has shown that people who eat too much food find greater satisfaction when eating from a smaller plate, even when they themselves have measured the same amounts of food onto a larger and a smaller plate. This may be partially an illusion, but why not use it to your advantage? See if it works for you. ❑

3. Slow down your eating. Overweight people usually eat too quickly. There is a time-lag between the stomach being full and the 'stop-eating' signal arriving in the brain. This means that, if you eat quickly, the signal that you have had enough comes too late, by which time you have eaten more than you really need. By slowing down your eating, you will actually eat less and yet feel perfectly satisfied. ❑

You can slow down your eating using the following methods:

a) Pay more attention to the taste, smell and texture of your food. Really concentrate on it. You will be able to eat more slowly, enjoy your food more and eat less. ❏

b) Put down your knife and fork more frequently, for example after every one to three mouthfuls. ❏

c) Count the number of mouthfuls you eat. Take a short rest period after a certain number (for example, after four mouthfuls). ❏

d) Put your knife and fork down and take a one- to two-minute break during the meal. ❏

e) Be the last person to finish each course of the meal. By using these slowing down methods for a few days, you will be able to change the automatic habit of eating rapidly. Try to make a game of it so that your mind is occupied and you can enjoy trying to be last at finishing and the slowest eater at the table. ❏

4. Leave a small amount of food on your plate every time you eat. This will help you break the bad habit of eating just because there is food in front of you, rather than because you really want it. ❏

If you decide to reduce the amount of food you eat at meal times, practise the various techniques outlined above (and perhaps think of some others) and use them every time you have a meal. These techniques will help you to gradually modify your behaviour.

2. Reducing snacking

1. Always eat three regular, planned meals a day. ❏

2. Carry a card with you and mark down every time you eat between meals. This is exactly the same procedure that you used when you were reducing your smoking. Becoming aware of how frequently you eat between meals is an important step in taking control over your behaviour. You may be surprised at just how often you do have snacks. You should include everything you eat, such as biscuits, sweets, and crisps. By charting and monitoring your snacks, you will be able to reduce their frequency. ❏

3. Devise some personal rules for snacking. ❏

One young ex-smoker began to consider herself a chocolate-bar addict and often ate three or four at a time. Janet felt as strongly about having them as she used to feel about cigarettes. She eliminated her addiction by following these three eating rules:

a) She allowed herself to buy only one chocolate bar at

a time. She could eat as many chocolate bars as she wanted but she could buy only one at a time. ❑

b) She allowed herself to eat it in only one place – the cafeteria at her workplace. ❑

c) She kept a reliable note of every one that she ate. Knowing that she could have an unlimited number of chocolate bars took away her fear of deprivation but, by following the rules, Janet successfully eliminated her 'pro-chocolate programming' that made her constantly eat them. By recording her consumption and allowing herself to eat in only one place, she regained control over her behaviour. If she had tried to use willpower by stopping eating chocolate bars completely, you can imagine what would have happened. She would have quickly broken down and perhaps given up trying to control her eating behaviour completely. ❑

4. Make up a set of your own personal rules for snacking concerning when, where, and on what you are allowed to snack. ❑

a) Decide exactly where you will allow yourself to snack and then only snack there. For example, you may decide that you will snack only in the dining room at home and in the staff room at work. Whatever you decide, write it down on the

Progress Chart provided (see Appendix C: Rules for Snacking). ❏

b) Decide exactly when you will allow yourself to snack (for example, only at particular times in the morning and afternoon). Whatever you decide, write it down on your Progress Chart. ❏

c) Decide exactly what you will allow yourself to snack on. Your aim should be to reduce the total number of calories you eat. You can change what you eat by choosing only low-calorie snacks. If you normally eat two cookies at morning coffee break, you may decide to eat just one low-calorie cookie. Or you may decide to switch to a different kind of very low-calorie snack, such as raw celery, cucumber, carrot, cauliflower, radishes or fruit such as oranges, plums, peaches, or apples. ❏

It may seem useless to make such small changes to your eating habits. However, given time, such little changes add up. By making small adjustments now, you will avoid developing a bigger weight problem later. Because they are only small adjustments to your eating behaviour, you should be able to incorporate them more easily into your daily routine.

3. Deprogramming unwanted eating habits

Just as having a cup of coffee sets off the desire to smoke in many people, so different triggers can produce a desire to eat. Obviously, you can't deprogram the desire to eat completely but, when something triggers the desire to eat at an inappropriate moment, you should do something about it if you want to have better control over your weight.

One woman realised that every time she walked past a sweet shop, she got a strong desire to eat something sugary. Without even thinking about it, she would just walk in and buy some sweets. A few moments beforehand she had had no desire for it; but, upon seeing the shop, she automatically went in and bought herself some. It didn't occur to her for over a year that the sight of the sweet shop was a very potent trigger to eat.

To deprogram your snacking triggers you can use the same three steps (Stop − Think − Deprogram) that have proved so helpful in stopping smoking. Every time you feel a desire to eat outside one of your permitted times, you should:

1. STOP
2. THINK What is the trigger? What's making you feel like eating? Notice if something is happening that is triggering the idea that you would like to eat something.
3. START DEPROGRAMMING Tell yourself in a firm, forceful way what you will do next time that trigger appears. For example, 'Just because I'm

walking past a shop that sells sweets doesn't mean I have to eat sweets. The next time I walk past a sweet shop, I don't want to automatically feel like eating sweet. Don't send me those eating triggers. I'll choose when, where, and what I'll eat.'

The Three Steps should be used for every one of your snacking triggers that occur outside of your agreed eating times. You may find that some of them are, in reality, old smoking triggers. Treat them in exactly the same way. Write a list of triggers in your Progress Chart (see Appendix A). Once you have completed your deprogramming, you will find that you will be less likely to experience a strong desire to nibble or eat the next time you are in that situation. If you still feel the desire to eat something, don't deprive yourself, but follow the rules for snacking you have set yourself as to what and how much you are going to eat. Remember, each time you deprogram yourself and follow your new rules, you are gaining more and more control over your behaviour. Take it gently and, above all, enjoy doing it. The more you enjoy doing it, the more often you will use the techniques, and thus the greater control you'll have over your own behaviour.

4. Alternative scenarios for trigger emotions

Many people have learned to cope with emotional situations by smoking or eating. For a compulsive smoker or eater, it is difficult to imagine not lighting up or not going to the refrigerator when feeling fed up, angry or bored. Smoking or eating when in a bad mood doesn't actually solve the problem that triggered the emotion in the first place, even though smokers and compulsive eaters often think that it helps – or that it is at least better than doing nothing. Unfortunately, in the long run, these unwanted habits can actually make you feel even worse. A little time spent considering alternative behaviour beforehand can be of great value in avoiding eating or smoking when an emotional crisis occurs. Emotional upsets of one sort or another are inevitable for all of us, but it is also inevitable that they will pass away in time. And, when they have passed, it is very disappointing indeed to find yourself smoking again or a few pounds heavier. Look over the following list of alternatives. As you read them, try to think of something more appropriate to do. Write down your ideas as you explore possibilities. As you read through the list, mark off those suggestions that you find particularly appealing or that you at least feel are worth a try. Add ideas of your own.

When you are in the grip of a negative emotion or feeling, it is so easy to say: 'What the hell! I don't care anymore. I feel so rotten; I don't care if I start smoking again or if I do get fat.' That kind of helpless, hopeless thinking is precisely what keeps people eating too much food and may even bring about a relapse of smoking. When the crisis passes, as it always does, you will be very pleased that you have prepared an alternative scenario to help you cope while you are down. Change the scenario. Write yourself a new script. Be your own person. Do it now! Feeling worried, angry, sad or lonely? When you are feeling any of these negative emotions, choose one of the following activities instead of eating, drinking, or smoking. Mark off any idea that you would like to try. While you are doing so, also consider the need to increase your activity level.

- Something physical

  ☐ exercise, for example:

  _____

  ☐ weed the garden
  ☐ clean your house, or

  _____

Physical exercise could have lots of positive benefits over and above helping keep your weight down; see Chapter 11 for further details.

- Use a relaxation technique for 20 minutes or so.

  ☐ relax to a CD you like
  ☐ meditate for twenty minutes (as your mind returns to thinking about your problems, gently go back to your mantra. Remember, meditation is about being rather than doing)
  ☐ take a hot, relaxing bath or

  _____

You may be surprised what a difference a little relaxation can make to the way you feel.

- Deliberately divert your attention from your feelings by imagining something pleasurable.

  ☐ think about a book you like
  ☐ think about a movie you saw recently and enjoyed
  ☐ think about a friend you particularly like
  ☐ think about an outing you enjoyed or

  _____

A technique like this may not solve your problem, but it helps to take the pressure off, helping you to be more rational, and less likely to eat or smoke.

- Do something pleasurable.

  ☐ read a book
  ☐ watch TV, a DVD or video
  ☐ visit or phone a friend
  ☐ go for a walk in the park
  ☐ involve yourself in a hobby or

  _____

When you feel bad, remember that it takes a conscious decision to deliberately make the effort to do one of these activities. It is easy to say to yourself, 'Reading won't do any good. It won't help the situation.' But remember that doing this is not intended to solve the problem; it will give you time out so you can handle the situation better.

- If your worry is caused by a specific problem try to talk it over with a supportive person, rather than simply do nothing other than eat or smoke.

5. Mentally rehearse your new eating behaviours

Having successfully stopped smoking, you have set in motion a number of different processes in your body and started a healthier lifestyle. Having got this far, it would be a great pity not to maintain your achievements and for this reason you should continue to use your imagination creatively. Your imagination – your thoughts, images and ideas – can control your behaviour as your new life develops. Your imagery provides a powerful method of practising new activities, ways of coping and changes in lifestyle.

When you settle down at night, ready for sleep, and begin to relax, this is a perfect time to work with your imagination. In the few minutes just before you drop off to sleep, think about what you have done during the day. Think of the things you have done with which you aren't entirely satisfied. Imagine how things might have been. By imagining yourself acting, behaving, eating, or drinking differently, you set into motion the very processes that will begin to change your behaviour. For example, you may remember that you felt hassled at work. Other people were bothering you and not letting you get on with what you really wanted to do. Almost automatically, your mind flashed on your cigarettes. Even now your old PCPs are lying dormant, still not completely eliminated. You went out and got yourself a packet of peppermints and ate the whole bag during the course of the afternoon, hardly in line with keeping your weight down.

As you lie in bed relaxing, think about the situation again. But this time imagine acting in a quite different manner. You might see yourself expressing your irritation directly to whoever it was that upset you. This is much more adaptive than going out to buy those peppermints. Or you might choose to see yourself taking a deep breath and eliminating the anger as you breathe out. See yourself doing this several times until, in your imagination, you can see yourself feeling calm again. Let your images do the work for you, by making them as real as possible. You can also use this time just before falling asleep to practise those techniques you have decided to use to control your eating. For example, if you have decided to leave a little food on your plate at every meal, imagine actually doing this. Imagine putting your knife and fork down, yet leaving a little food on the plate. You can prepare yourself and get used to the idea that you don't have to eat everything. Imagine that this has become a quite normal and regular thing to do. Anticipate the comments your family might make and how you would explain to them what you are doing.

By choosing what to do in your imagination, you can begin to train your mind. Remember that there is always an alternative to eating, drinking and smoking in response to negative emotions. By imagining yourself acting in new ways, you are actually writing new programs into your Biocomputer. Your images provide new action plans and new models for your behaviour. By deliberately building new 'memories' of yourself acting differently, you will be surprised to find yourself acting in new ways, more or less automatically and spontaneously. If you mentally practise doing some exercise instead of going to the refrigerator when you feel sad, you will find that the next time you do feel sad, the chances of actually doing some exercise, rather than eating, will be greater.

The principal guideline is to make any change in your behaviour slowly and gradually. Although your imagery might be quite powerful and make you feel capable of managing almost anything, don't demand too much at any one time and don't try to see yourself making dramatic changes overnight. Do not try to reprogram yourself with things like, 'From tomorrow onwards I will not eat between meals,' because it simply won't be possible that quickly. If you eat between meals very often, you will end up being disappointed when you fail to maintain your decision every single time a trigger appears.

Willpower is no more useful now than it was giving up smoking. Imagine yourself changing gradually, slowly getting better and better, changing your behaviour systematically and surely, rather than doing it all in a rush and being defeated.

Let's consider this example. Since stopping smoking, suppose that you have developed the habit of eating peppermints all day. Instead of cutting them out all at once, use mental rehearsal to imagine eating them only at certain times or making a packet last two days instead of one. By making slow changes and nothing too dramatic, you are more likely to succeed progressively, until you find you are eating peppermints only occasionally. By cutting them out all at once, you increase your chances of failing, becoming discouraged and then not bothering to try any more. You can achieve remarkable things if you use your imagination to plan action in a systematic fashion.

Summary

- The same methods that helped you to stop smoking can be applied to your eating and drinking if they become a problem.
- Your weight can be controlled in two ways: by reducing your consumption of fattening food and by increasing your bodily activity. By eating healthier food and taking more exercise, your weight will normalise.
- Go through the targets A–J listed in the chapter and set yourself three priorities. Work towards achieving these targets, one after the other.
- Select those methods that you find most useful or appealing personally. Small changes made slowly are more successful than large changes made quickly.
- Use imagery rehearsal and the three steps to reduce snacking between meals and to change your eating habits.
- Whatever else you do, remember that smoking is a thing of the past. Take one day at a time and your

weight can be slowly but surely restored to its pre-quit level.

- Continue to enhance your general well-being and enjoyment of life by maintaining your programme of relaxation.

11

Becoming more active

When smokers quit, a major change occurs in the pattern of their activity. A typical twenty-five-a-day smoker takes around a hundred thousand puffs per year from over nine thousand cigarettes. The total time taken up by smoking is the equivalent of one whole month out of every year. Smokers also tend to do less physical exercise than non-smokers. Stopping smoking therefore may create an activity gap and a time gap that need to be filled. This chapter contains guidelines on how these gaps can be filled by adding new activities into daily routines.

For many people, neither problem will be all that serious. Other things, for which there hadn't previously been enough time, simply fill the gap left by smoking. Smoking is something that is often not done on its own. However, for those who smoked a lot of the time while alone, there will be a noticeable gap to fill. It is for this group that this chapter will be especially useful. Increased physical activity can benefit anybody looking for ideas to improve their general well-being.

The fidget factor

Smokers fall into two types – those for whom the effects of nicotine are most important ('Nicotine Missers') and those who see smoking as an important way of filling gaps in their daily activities ('Fidgeter Types'). Which type are you? Misser or Fidgeter? When Fidgeters quit smoking, they need to have something else to do with their hands and also, possibly, their mouths. Activities such as fidgeting, doodling, tapping or twiddling small objects may be useful especially during the first few weeks. You could buy a stress ball made of soft foam or rubber to keep in your hand or a pocket; a squash ball would serve the same purpose. It's quieter than playing with a bunch of keys that may irritate others. Worry beads may also provide a useful substitute.

Oral activities that have proved helpful for new non-smokers include chewing gum, sipping fruit juice or water and teeth-gritting. Some ex-smokers feel fidgety and restless and constantly move or jiggle about. If you find yourself with this feeling, you'll probably automatically be doing one or more of the activities listed above. Your Chimp restlessness will eventually die down to tolerable levels. There are also ways your new energies can be channelled into beneficial activities and physical exercise.

Physical exercise

Most people take far less exercise than is desirable from a health point of view. The passive viewing of TV has taken over as the dominant form of social and recreational activity. The couch potato who stops smoking is therefore more likely to experience the restless, empty feeling than those who are physically active and will need to avoid eating to fill the gap (see Chapter 10 for more details). It's also a good idea to consider starting an exercise plan.

Regular exercise enhances mood, reduces depression and anxiety and generally leads to increased well-being. A personal exercise programme will help you to fill any activity gap and will also raise your general level of fitness. All these factors provide a clear bonus for your physical health.

Exercise: why bother?

1. Exercise helps you feel good.
2. It's great fun and a good way of making new friends and enjoying your leisure time more.
3. It helps you feel more energetic.
4. It helps you relax.
5. It helps you get slim and stay slim.
6. It helps keep you supple and, as you get older, more mobile.
7. It helps strengthen your muscles, joints and even your bones.
8. It helps your heart work more efficiently and improves your circulation.
9. It needn't cost anything.
10. The more you do, the easier it becomes.

What is fitness?

Suppleness

This means being able to bend, stretch, twist and turn through a full range of movement. You need it for awkward jobs around the house and getting in and out of different forms of transportation. If you're supple, you're less likely to get injured and you'll be able to stay more active as you get older.

Strength

This means being able to exert force – push, pull and lift. You need strength to move around, carry shopping bags, climb upstairs and take stubborn tops off bottles! Strength protects your body from sprains and strains. A strong back and stomach will improve your posture, too.

Stamina

This means being able to keep going when walking briskly or engaging in other forms of activity, without getting tired or out of breath very quickly. Stamina is useful when you're in a hurry to get somewhere or when you need to keep up with your children! Exercising for stamina helps to protect you against heart disease. The best activities for stamina are those that are more energetic than you are used to doing, that make you slightly out of breath and that keep you moving for twenty minutes or more. This type of exercise is often called 'aerobic' exercise, because it makes you breathe in enough oxygen to supply your working muscles. Lots of the activities in this chapter fall into this group.

Are you willing to exercise?

There are a lot of excuses you could use to avoid exercise – but they're very easily answered.

- 'It's too much hard work. I'd never keep it up.' It won't seem like hard work if you choose an exercise you enjoy and build up the length of exercise time and intensity slowly and gradually. As you get better, you'll enjoy it even more and you won't want to give it up.
- 'I haven't got time. My life is too busy.' Just twenty minutes, two or three times a week, can keep you active. Once you start feeling the benefits and your new activity becomes a habit, it'll be easy to put aside the time.
- 'What I need is relaxation.' Exercise can be just the thing to help you relax. It relieves stress by talking your mind off your problems. After a session of vigorous exercise, you'll feel warm, comfortable and relaxed. You'll notice the relaxing effect of some kinds of exercise even while you're doing them. Recent studies have shown that exercising can also lift depression. You'll probably find it helps you sleep better, too.

- 'But doesn't it have to hurt to do you any good?' No. If it hurts, then you're pushing yourself too hard. If you're in any pain, stop immediately. If you feel uncomfortably out of breath, slow down.

- 'It's too late for me – I'm past it!' It's never too late. Anyone can get fitter. Whatever your age, you can find a form of exercise that will suit you. The less fit you are to start with, the sooner you'll notice the benefits.

- 'But isn't it bad for my heart?' On the contrary, it helps to protect your heart. When you exercise, your muscles need more oxygen than usual, so your heart has to beat faster to pump more oxygen-carrying blood to them. If you exercise regularly, your muscles get better at using oxygen and your heart pumps more blood with each beat, so it doesn't need to beat so fast. As you get fitter, you can exercise harder without overtaxing your heart. *Regular* exercise has other benefits too. It can help to control high blood pressure. It can also help stop your arteries furring up. Over the years, your risk of having a heart attack will be reduced.

- 'I'm not the sporty type.' Even if you didn't like sports at school, there are now so many different activities, you are sure to be able to find one you enjoy. Just try different ones until you find the one that's right for you.

- 'I couldn't do it on my own.' You don't have to. Clubs and classes are really good places to make friends and lots of them have social events as well as exercise. Why not show this chapter to your friends and get them to go along with you?

- 'I'd be too embarrassed.' Don't let embarrassment put you off exercise – you'd be missing out on too much. People of all shapes and sizes enjoy exercising and you won't feel uncomfortable or out of place if you choose an activity that's right for you.

- 'I couldn't bear all the sprains and strains.' You'll only get these if you push yourself too hard, too soon or if you do occasional sessions of hard exercise and nothing in between. If you start off gently and build up slowly, your risk of developing a sprain or strain is very low. Exercise also builds up strong muscles that protect you from injury. When muscles aren't used, for example when a broken leg is put in a cast, the muscles waste away and the leg gets thin and weak. When muscles are used more than usual, the opposite happens: they become stronger and more efficient.

- 'I've got young children to look after.' It might take a bit more organising, but it doesn't have to stop you exercising. Some sports centres have childcare facilities. Your local library should be able to tell you about facilities. Or you could get together with a group of other people with young children and share the babysitting.

- 'If I can't do it properly, then what's the point of doing it at all?' You don't have to go into serious training and get super-fit or play competitive sports to benefit from exercise. Regular activity for just twenty or thirty minutes, two or three times a week, will go a long way towards helping you stay in good shape.

- 'I'm too fat for that kind of thing.' Then you are just the sort of person who will benefit most from some regular exercise, especially if it's the stamina-building type. Most people don't need a medical check-up before starting to exercise. Exercising helps you get slim and stay slim by burning calories. If you burn more calories than you eat, your body will start using its own energy stores and fat will start to disappear. There's evidence that some people may still be burning up more calories than usual after they have finished exercising – sometimes for several hours.

Before you start

Sensible precautions

As long as you choose the right form of exercise, begin gently and increase the length and intensity of your exercise session gradually, you'll gain all the benefits without straining yourself. Always warm up first, with a few gentle bends and stretches and cool down afterwards by walking slowly for a few minutes. Most injuries are caused by overuse of joints and muscles, so don't overdo it. In general, don't do anything vigorous unless you have built up to that level of intensity and you do it regularly.

Always ask your doctor about the best form of exercise for you if:

- You've had chest pains, high blood pressure or heart disease.
- You have chest trouble, such as asthma or bronchitis.
- You have back trouble or have had a slipped disc.
- You have joint pains or arthritis.
- You have diabetes.
- You're recovering from an illness or operation.
- You're worried that exercise may affect any other aspects of your health.

For all these conditions listed above, exercise can be helpful, but it is a good idea to talk it over with your doctor first.

If you are over the age of thirty-five, you should have your blood pressure checked by your doctor or at a clinic at least once a year, whether or not you intend to take up exercise.

Having a disability doesn't mean you shouldn't exercise. You may benefit from regular exercise of the right kind.

If you're pregnant, there's no reason why you shouldn't continue with any sport or activity you already enjoy. Exercising in pregnancy is beneficial as long as you feel comfortable. However, do not start new exercise programmes when you're pregnant.

If you have a cold, a temperature or a sore throat, don't exercise until you feel better and remember to start gradually when you get back into it. Don't do any vigorous exercise for at least an hour after a meal.

Stop exercising immediately if you have any of these symptoms:

- pain
- dizziness
- a feeling of being sick or unwell
- unusual fatigue

If the symptoms persist or come back later or if you are worried about them, see your doctor.

Clothes and footwear

For most activities, you won't need to buy anything new. Just wear loose, comfortable clothes and a good strong pair of shoes. For any activity that involves a lot of running or jumping you will need a good pair of running shoes to protect your feet, joints and back from damage. Make sure the shoes you buy have a thick, cushioned sole, especially at the heel, to prevent jarring of your joints. Check that the sole is wide enough for comfort, with plenty of room for your toes. Look for shoes with a good arch support and strong heel cup; this will stop your foot tilting inwards while you're running.

Remember you may need a size larger than your normal shoes, because your feet are likely to spread a little when you exercise and you may be wearing thicker socks than usual.

Getting started

If you're not very active now, your first step to getting fitter is simply to walk more. Why stand at a bus stop or sit in a traffic jam when, with a bit of effort, you can walk or cycle all or part of a journey almost as quickly?

When you walk, walk faster. Walking briskly for twenty to thirty minutes, two or three times a week, will soon build up your stamina.

Use the stairs instead of the elevator, and walk up escalators. Climbing stairs is a good way of keeping your leg muscles strong. Even if you are active at home or at work, you'll probably still need other activities to give you enough suppleness, strength and stamina. You'll find activities listed below that will give you a good balance.

Four golden rules of Exercise

Get moving

Use more effort than usual by finding a more active way to do the things you usually do and by taking up completely new activities. Move through a wider range of movements and keep going for longer.

Build up gradually

It takes time to get fit. Work hard enough to make yourself a bit sweaty and out of breath, but not uncomfortably so. That way, there will also be a lower risk of sprains and strains. Always warm up first, with a few gentle bends and stretches and cool down afterwards by walking slowly for a few minutes.

Exercise regularly

It'll take twenty to thirty minutes of exercise two or three times a week for you to get fit and stay fit.

Keep it up

You can't store fitness.

Activities

There are hundreds of activities to choose from. Choose activities that

- you enjoy.
- make you feel good.
- you can do regularly – for twenty or thirty minutes, two or three times a week.
- you can fit easily into your everyday routine, so there's no excuse for not keeping them up.
- you can do near home, so you don't have to travel far.
- don't depend on the weather or seasons.
- suit your particular fitness needs.

Here are some ideas to choose from:

- Walking
- Swimming
- Bicycling
- Jogging and running
- Golf
- Bowling
- Badminton
- Tennis
- Squash or racquetball
- Team games
- Weight training
- Martial arts and judo
- Exercise classes
- Dance
- Exercising at home
- Yoga

Summary

- Get fit and stay fit! Once you're fit, you need to make sure you stay fit. Once you start becoming habitually active, staying fit won't seem difficult.
- The way to get fitter is to be more active and vigorous than you usually are.
- Try to choose the active ways of doing daily tasks, instead of the lazy ways. You'll be surprised what difference small changes can make to your fitness.

- Choose a form of exercise you enjoy enough to do regularly, for at least twenty to thirty minutes, two or three times a week and make a habit of it.
- Whatever you choose to do, start gently and build up gradually. You don't have to strain yourself to feel the benefits of exercise.
- You don't have to choose just one thing. Try lots of different activities, to give you a good balance of suppleness, strength and stamina. Have fun!

12

Life skills for the
ex-smoker

This final chapter focuses on the psychological aspects of becoming a successful non-smoker. You have the awareness and skills necessary for coping with the traps and pitfalls that may be set by others. However, anybody who tries to break your resolve by tempting you with cigarettes or giving you a hard time, is really on the defensive. You need to be in charge and make your own choices, rather than have them imposed on you by other people and events.

It is important at this stage to develop your strategies for minimising the risk of relapse. Some of the more significant, longer-term factors in changing your lifestyle have been covered in the preceding chapters. You also need to be on your guard against momentary slips or lapses that could take you unawares and push you back into your earlier groove of smoking. To help you avoid this, here is a list of the key danger points.

Preventing relapse

The biggest task for you as an ex-smoker is preventing lapses or slips. This is because any slip can lead to full-blown re-lapse. It is necessary to guard against this, to be on the alert for high-risk situations. The major danger points are:

- Negative emotional states and mood swings: frustra-tion, anxiety, depression, boredom, or loneliness. Ways of coping with these moods swings and feelings without smoking, eating, or drinking are described in some detail in Chapter 6.
- Positive emotional states: success, joy, happiness and good company. Fortunately, you're less likely to lapse when you're in a positive mood than when you're in a negative mood, but lapses can still happen. All that can really be said here is: don't spoil it by smoking.
- Social pressure: this can be direct, for example when somebody offers you a cigarette or indirect, for example when you're in the company of smokers at a party and you end up asking somebody for a cigarette. This is discussed in more detail on page 292 below.
- Conflict/stress: this can occur almost anywhere but the key situations are at work and at home. Forty to fifty per cent of all relapses are attributed to stress. You must learn to deal with stressful situations with-out relying on a cigarette. Suggestions about how to do this are provided in Chapter 6. It will also help you if you remember and understand some of the basic characteristics of smokers.

Understanding smokers

You can easily understand smokers because, only recently, you were one! You could even admit that you still are a potential smoker. Smokers are one of the biggest external influences on your success or failure, but only if you let them be. Some smokers may even attempt to sabotage your best efforts to remain a non-smoker and you need to be prepared to deal with them. You have successfully completed the first stage of becoming a non-smoker and it is vital that you remain a non-smoker for the rest of your life. You can achieve this in spite of Pro-Cigarette Programs (PCPs) or smokers trying to back-slide you out of your non-smoking groove into your old groove as a smoker. The power of your very-much-weakened PCPs, which could still be lying dormant somewhere inside your Biocomputer, needs to be continually monitored, as does the potential influence of smokers you run into in everyday life. The way you deal with them could make all the difference to your long-term success.

For many, smoking is a key part of their life, a tool for changing bad moods into good, for relaxing or being active and for a hundred other momentary purposes. Smoking accompanies practically everything that the smoker does from the first to the last waking moment each day, and permeates everything the smoker comes into contact with, thinks about or has a feeling about. Stopping and starting things, having a conversation, eating, drinking, thinking or simply doing nothing in particular, are all associated with smoking.

In some cases, smokers will go to incredible lengths to keep cigarette smoke in their lungs. The city where I once lived in New Zealand, Dunedin, is situated at the end of a beautiful harbour. For several miles, the road runs right beside the sea, only a few feet below. One summer, three different smokers drove into the harbour as a result of dropping lit cigarettes between their legs onto the driver's seat!

I once met a lung surgeon who had spent thirty years removing lungs and tumours from patients suffering from one of the worst and most painful conditions caused by smoking: lung cancer. I could hardly believe it when the surgeon took out a packet of cigarettes, offered me one and admitted that he was a twenty-five-a-day smoker!

Many smokers are almost totally dominated by the quest for nicotine and the majority like to smoke in company whenever possible. Doing something in a crowd makes it feel more acceptable. You need to be constantly on guard because the smoker may strike when you least expect it. Watch out for the feel-good factor, when you feel as if you can cope with anything. Smoking and drinking tend to go together and so you will be most at risk in situations where alcohol flows.

Something like 50 to 60 per cent of all lapses occur as a result of obtaining a cigarette from another smoker. In many cases, the lapse occurs while alcohol, food, tea or coffee are being consumed and smokers just fall back into their old ways. As an ex-smoker, you may not behave or think rationally, as far as your smoking is concerned, for several months or years following quitting. Once a smoker you are always a smoker, potentially. Your smoking friends may therefore unwittingly put you at risk simply by smoking in your company. One key to successful relapse prevention is to learn to manage social situations where eating and drinking occurs in the company of smokers.

Assertiveness

So how should you handle smokers if they try to reconvert you? You need to listen carefully to what they say and, if necessary, treat it with a pinch of salt. Assert your right to not smoke. Smokers need to accept and respect your views too. Sometimes it can be quite tricky. For example, you're outside at a party and people next to you are smoking without a care in the world. The key concept to remember is that you and you alone are in charge of your mind and body. Assert this right whenever there is any doubt about the matter. Assert your right not to smoke and not to inhale passively the smoke of others.

If the worst comes to the worst, you may have to move away rather than deal with an ugly confrontation. The best way to deal with this is a matter of judgement but you can be artful about this and avoid unwanted smoke without getting a slap or a bloody nose.

Managing time

For many people, life seems to be speeding up: there is little time to plan or think or 'chill out'. Everybody these days is talking about stress – the stress of working, the stress of commuting, stress from the family, or simply the stress of living – but it is an abused and misapplied term that is rarely properly defined. Everybody thinks that they automatically know what stress is. However, it is a term that even so-called 'experts' often do not define in any clear or meaningful way.

Most uses of the term 'stress' would be better served by the term 'strain', following the original concepts in engineering. Strain is what occurs in an object when stresses are placed upon it. The stress of a hurricane may cause too great a strain on a busy suspension bridge and lead to its collapse. 'Stress' is a property of the hurricane (the surrounding environment) and 'strain' a property of the bridge (the human being).

Recent theories have looked at the relationship between the resources of a person and the demands placed on those resources in the course of everyday living. When a person's resources are insufficient to meet the demands placed upon them, strain is the inevitable result. A person's resources consist of everything they have for the process of living, whether material (money and tangible assets), psychological (knowledge, abilities and skills) or social (support from family, friends and colleagues). All three factors contribute in making a change when it is as big as quitting smoking for life.

One of the most important resources is time. Like any other, it is finite and the way it is used can prevent or provoke strain. By carefully planning how you use your time, you will have more control over your well-being. One of the greatest stressors is having too little time to finish the things you believe that you need to get done. Managing time is therefore closely linked with your ability to say 'No'. When excessive demands are placed upon you, whether at work or at home, you need to be clear about what you can and cannot manage in the time available. This requires sitting down and planning carefully how long each task is going to take and how many other things you need to do within a particular timescale. The thing to remember is that we always underestimate how long things really do take. A good rule of thumb is to add 50 per cent to the time you allow to do things, just to be on the safe side of the stress–strain equation.

One of the most effective ways of reducing strain is to take on only those things that you know you can complete within the time available. Timetables are therefore essential. If you don't have one already, buy a diary that has enough space to schedule your days by the hour. Plan when and where you are going and what you are going to do. Leave days free for essential things you know you normally have a problem fitting in. Cancel or postpone activities that are of low priority and things that you know you cannot fit in. Always allow enough time for any necessary preparation and for any follow-up activities that may be required afterwards (e.g. reports, letters, emails, telephone calls or for just letting everything 'gel').

Time management has a lot to do with privacy and not being available at certain times so that you can attend to your own needs for relaxation and care, both mentally and physically. Routines are very helpful, so that others can learn when you will be available for certain activities and when you will be unavailable. Accessibility is a key factor. If you have never thought about these issues before, now would be an excellent time to take stock of what your duties, responsibilities, and needs really are. When you have considered them carefully, you will want to negotiate with others who might be affected by what the new 'accessibility' rules are going to be. Others among family, friends and colleagues will need to adjust their expectations and timetables accordingly.

Your preferences may sometimes conflict with those of others, so you will need to negotiate a way of dealing with the problem. Aim for a compromise that leaves everybody feeling happy about what is planned for your future time together. Give yourself the best chance of minimising avoidable strains resulting from poor time management.

Relaxation

One of your best long-term strategies as a confirmed non-smoker will be to ensure you have plenty of relaxation. Make relaxation a central part of your daily, weekly and monthly routines. As a non-smoker you will have more money, more time and more energy. Why not develop a new interest or pastime to enhance your enjoyment of life and promote relaxation?

As we saw in Chapter 11, physical leisure activities can provide an important source of relaxation as the mind is given the chance to take itself away from everyday worries and concerns. It doesn't really matter which form of relaxation you choose but, if you can combine mental relaxation with physical activity, it will be even more beneficial.

Controlling stress and strain

Stress, strain, and how to control them has almost fomed a new religion. Google, YouTube, Facebook and Twitter, tablets, smartphones and TV have replaced prayers to God and confessionals for advice on how to live. Internet gurus are the new prophets. But you should avoid the smoke and mirrors. Be critical. Challenge what you see. The greatest power to control the stress and strain in your life lies inside you. You and you alone can fix it.

As a non-smoker, you have taken control of your body from the automatic programming that kept you smoking. This major change symbolises a whole new approach to your methods of dealing and coping with stress and strain. It gives you a completely new identity in which you make the decisions about your life. Smoking had become a great stress to you, but that is now in your past. This book has provided you with a powerful set of methods that you can use to eliminate all of the other stresses in your everyday life.

Although people who lapse into smoking give many different reasons for restarting the habit, what is called 'stress' is by far the most common. Stress can take the form of unexpected or tragic life events such as accidents, deaths or family illnesses or it may consist of arguments, separations, divorces, redundancies or other events that pose a major threat to personal security. These events are often unpredicted, unplanned, and unrehearsed. You need to build up your personal reserves to be better equipped to deal with potential threats. You can build up your reserves using all of the methods suggested in Part Two of this book. In addition, greater physical fitness toughens you both physically and mentally. If you are worried about your weight, learning to control your eating habits and taking more exercise will help you to correct the problem. Relaxation, meditation and the practice of being, rather than doing, are key strategies for protecting yourself from avoidable strain. The methods in this book offer you protective tools and techniques for the enhancement of your well-being.

One of the greatest factors is the power of your thinking to influence the way you see things in the first place. This is really the old division between pessimists and optimists. 'For there is nothing either good or bad but thinking makes it so.' Today, psychologists are investigating how the explanations people give for the events in their lives reflect optimistic or pessimistic thinking styles. While optimists treat stress as a challenge and live to fight another day, pessimists see almost everything as a problem and find everything simply too much to cope with.

Stress and strain can never be eliminated altogether. Life is impossible without stress. Indeed, a life without challenges would be very dull one indeed. What we can all learn to do better is not to allow unavoidable events to immobilise us, blocking the creative processes of growth, development, and recovery. The next chapter in life's unfolding story is always there, waiting to begin. The success that you achieve in quitting smoking for life will make a positive contribution to your well-being, both physical and psychological and to your self-belief. You can continue to work on your improved sense of well-being through meditation and mindfulness.

Using the tools provided here, you can successfully change not only your behaviour but your life experience as a person. The methods are simple to apply and quite general in their application. If you continue to use them when needed, you can give yourself an excellent chance of successfully stopping smoking for good. You can adapt the methods as you wish. Be creative and achieve other objectives in your life. In this way, you can continue to improve your well-being.

Being is as important as doing. Being calm is as important as being busy. Stop. . . think . . . what is the trigger for the stress in your life? Use the tools you now possess in your armoury to good purpose. Your well-being and the well-being of your loved ones are paramount. The mind is the most powerful instrument you have. By meditating, living in the present, using mindfulness, being in the moment, breathing beautiful fresh air, you will become a new person. It is natural and free to be mindful. It is natural and free to manage your thoughts, feelings and behaviours.

Summary

- Be on your guard against high-risk situations.
- Manage your time as efficiently as possible so that you are less pressured by other people and events.
- Set aside time on a regular basis purely for your own relaxation, including meditation.
- Develop a new interest or hobby to add to the quality of your life.
- Manage stress by preventing it to begin with.
- Live in the present.
- Remember the profoundly wise words of the bard: 'For there is nothing either good or bad but thinking makes it so.'
- Live and enjoy your new nicotine-free life to the full.

Abbreviations

ACPs – Anti-Cigarette Programs

CBT – Cognitive Behavioural Therapy

CHD – Coronary heart disease

COPD – Chronic obstructive pulmonary disease

ETS – Environmental tobacco smoke

FDA – Food and Drug Administration (US)

MAO – Monoamineoxidase

MDS – Mesolimbic dopamine system

MHRA – The Medicines and Healthcare products Regulatory Agency (UK)

MBCT – Mindfulness-Based Cognitive Therapy

NO – Nitrous oxide

NRT – Nicotine Replacement Therapy

PCPs – Pro-Cigarette Programs

PPCAs – Phoney Pro-Cigarette Arguments

SIDS – Sudden Infant Death Syndrome

WHO – World Health Organization

WOT – Withdrawal-Oriented therapy

Useful references and websites

Sources on nicotine addiction and health

Let's Make the Next Generation Tobacco-free: Your guide to the 50th Anniversary Surgeon General's Report on Smoking and Health (2014), www.surgeongeneral.gov/library/reports/50-years-of-progress/consumer-guide.pdf

The Health Consequences of Smoking – Fifty Years of Progress: A Report of the Surgeon General 2014, US Department of Health and Human Services, Public Health Service Office of the Surgeon General Rockville, MD, www.surgeongeneral.gov/library/reports/50-years-of-progress/full-report.pdf

'Chronic Smoking-Related Lung Disease Blights Over One Million Lives in England', Public Health England, 2015, www.gov.uk/government/news/chronic-smoking-related-lung-disease-blights-over-1-million-lives-in-england

Statistics on smoking, www.hscic.gov.uk/lifestyles http://content.digital.nhs.uk/media/18659/Smoking-fact-sheet/pdf/HSCIC_Stoptober_infographic_A3_0915a.pdf

'More than one in ten babies born to mothers who smoke, 18 June 2015, www.hscic.gov.uk/article/6465/More-than-one-in-10-babies-born-to-mothers-who-smoke

Young People and Smoking, ASH Fact Sheet. July 2015, http://ash.org.uk/files/documents/ASH_108.pdf

Action on Smoking and Health (ASH), http://ash.org.uk/home/

Centers for Disease Control and Prevention (CDC), www.cdc.gov/

National Institute on Drug Abuse (NIDA), www.drugabuse.gov/

WhyQuit.Com, http://whyquit.com/

Stop Smoking Now, The Process (Facebook page), www.facebook.com/StopSmokingNowTheProcess/

Publications relevant to Stop Smoking Now

S. Casswell & D. Marks, 'Cannabis induced impairment of performance of a divided attention task,' *Nature,* 1973, 241, 60–61

S. Casswell & D. F. Marks, 'Cannabis and temporal disintegration in experienced and naive subjects', *Science,* 1973, 179, 4075, 803–805

M. G. MacAvoy & D. F. Marks, 'Divided attention performance of cannabis users and non-users following cannabis and alcohol' *Psychopharmacologia,* 1975, 44.2, 147–152

P. Sulzberger & D. Marks, *The Isis Smoking Cessation Programme*, Dunedin, New Zealand, 1977, 1978, 1979

Heylen Research Centre, 'Isis smoking cessation groups assessment study', Auckland, New Zealand, 1979

D. F. Marks & M. G. MacAvoy, 'Divided attention performance in cannabis users and non-users following alcohol and cannabis separately and in combination,' *Psychopharmacology,* 1989, 99.3, 397–401

D. F. Marks, 'Smoking cessation as a test-bed for psychological theory: a group cognitive therapy programme with high long-term abstinence rates', *The Journal of Smoking-Related Disorders*, 1992, 3, 69–78

D. F. Marks, 'Health psychology', *Current Opinion in Psychiatry,* 1992, 5(6):845–8

D. F. Marks, *The Quit for Life Programme: An Easier Way to Stop Smoking and Not Start Again,* 1993, the British Psychological Society

C. Haslam, E. S. Draper & E. Goyder, 'The pregnant smoker: a preliminary investigation of the social and psychological influences', *Journal of Public Health,* 1997, 19, 187–92

D. F. Marks, 'Addiction, smoking and health: developing policy-based interventions', *Psychology, Health and Medicine,* 1998, 3, 97–111

E. Kals, '*The Quit for Life Programme: An Easier Way to Stop*

Smoking and Not Start Again, (D. F. Marks; Leicester: the British Psychological Society, 1993)', book review in *Psychology and Health*, 1998, 13, 560–561

D. F. Marks, 'Supplement on smoking cessation incompletely discloses conflicts of interest, duplicates prior publication and advocates the pharmaceutical products of the sponsoring company in a potentially misleading manner', *European Journal of Public Health,* 2001

C. M. Sykes & D. F. Marks, 'Effectiveness of a cognitive behaviour therapy self-help programme for smokers in London, UK', *Health Promotion International*, 2001, *16*, 255–260

A. Parrott, 'Smoking cessation counselling', *New Directions in Counselling*, 2002, 3:154

D. F. Marks & C. M. Sykes, 'Randomised controlled trial of cognitive behavioural therapy for smokers living in a deprived area of london: outcome at one-year follow-up', *Psychology, Health & Medicine,* 2002, 7, 17–24

D. F. Marks & L. Yardley (eds.), *Research Methods for Clinical & Health Psychology*, 2004, SAGE Publications

D. F. Marks, *Overcoming Your Smoking Habit: A Self-Help Guide Using Cognitive Behavioural Techniques,* 2005, Robinson

K. H. Ginzel, G. S. Maritz, D. F. Marks, M. Neuberger, J. R. Pauly, J. R. Polito, R. Schulte-Hermann & T. A. Slotkin, 'Critical review: nicotine for the foetus, the infant and the adolescent?', *Journal of Health Psychology*, 2007, 12, 215–24

S. Michie, K. Jochelson, W. A. Markham & C. Bridle, 'Low income groups and behaviour change interventions:

a review of intervention content, effectiveness and theoretical frameworks', *Journal of Epidemiology and Community Health,* 21 April 2009

J. Bryant, B. Bonevski, C. Paul, P. McElduff & J. Attia, 'A systematic review and meta-analysis of the effectiveness of behavioural smoking cessation interventions in selected disadvantaged groups. *Addiction,* 2011, 106, 1568–85

N. Lindson-Hawley, P. Aveyard & J. R. Hughes, 'Reduction versus abrupt cessation in smokers who want to quit', *The Cochrane Library*, 2012

D. F. Marks, 'Health Psychology: Overview', *Handbook of Psychology, Vol. 9*, 2012, 3–25, John Wiley

E. R. Bull, S. U. Dombrowski, N. McCleary & M. Johnston, 'Are interventions for low-income groups effective in changing healthy eating, physical activity and smoking behaviours? A systematic review and meta-analysis,' *BMJ Open*, 2014, 4(11):e006046

D. F. Marks, M. Murray, & E. V. Estacio, *Health Psychology: Theory, Research and Practice,* (fifth ed.), 2018, SAGE Publications Ltd

D. F. Marks, 'Dyshomeostasis, obesity, addiction and chronic stress' *Health Psychology Open*, 2016, 3, 1

M. de Bruin et al., 'Identifying effective behavioural components of Intervention and Comparison group support provided in smoking cessation (IC-SMOKE) interventions: a systematic review protocol', *Systematic Reviews*, 2016, 5, 77

D. F. Marks, *Stop Smoking Now: The Process,* 2017, Yin and Yang Books

Appendix A

Progress Chart (Smoking)

Use this Chart to monitor your progress until you reach your D-Day. Your consumption should be added to the Progress Chart at the end of each 24-hour period.

Progress Chart (Smoking)

Use this Chart to monitor your progress until you reach your D-Day. It shows the reductions in consumption which has been obtained using this Programme. Your consumption should be added to the Progress Chart at the end of each 24-hour period. Note that the scale is measured in percentages of your original consumption level.

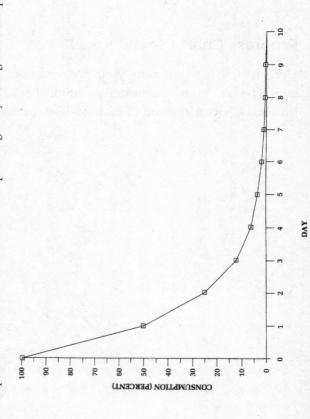

Appendix B

Daily Reduction 'Cards'

Use the 'cards' printed on this page and the next page to record every cigarette, or part of a cigarette, you smoke during the Programme. It is recommended that you photocopy the page and cut out the cards with a pair of scissors. Please use a new card each day to cover a 24-hour period. The 9 cards will last until your D-Day. Keep each card inside your cigarette packet and remember to record every cigarette you smoke. Write your total for every 24-hour period on your Progress Chart.

DAY 1 a.m. NURD p.m.		
12–1		
1–2		
2–3		
3–4		
4–5		
5–6		
6–7		
7–8		
8–9		
9–10		
10–11		
11–12		

DAY 2 a.m. NURD p.m.		
12–1		
1–2		
2–3		
3–4		
4–5		
5–6		
6–7		
7–8		
8–9		
9–10		
10–11		
11–12		

DAY 3 a.m. NURD p.m.		
12–1		
1–2		
2–3		
3–4		
4–5		
5–6		
6–7		
7–8		
8–9		
9–10		
10–11		
11–12		

DAY 4 a.m. NURD p.m.		
12–1		
1–2		
2–3		
3–4		
4–5		
5–6		
6–7		
7–8		
8–9		
9–10		
10–11		
11–12		

DAY 5 a.m. NURD p.m.		
12–1		
1–2		
2–3		
3–4		
4–5		
5–6		
6–7		
7–8		
8–9		
9–10		
10–11		
11–12		

DAY 6 a.m. NURD p.m.		
12–1		
1–2		
2–3		
3–4		
4–5		
5–6		
6–7		
7–8		
8–9		
9–10		
10–11		
11–12		

	DAY 7 a.m. NURD p.m.	
12–1		
1–2		
2–3		
3–4		
4–5		
5–6		
6–7		
7–8		
8–9		
9–10		
10–11		
11–12		

	DAY 8 a.m. NURD p.m.	
12–1		
1–2		
2–3		
3–4		
4–5		
5–6		
6–7		
7–8		
8–9		
9–10		
10–11		
11–12		

	DAY 9 a.m. NURD p.m.	
12–1		
1–2		
2–3		
3–4		
4–5		
5–6		
6–7		
7–8		
8–9		
9–10		
10–11		
11–12		

Appendix C

Progress Chart (Eating)

Use this Progress Chart to monitor your success in keeping to your Personal Eating Rules. Write the three techniques you decided to use in the space provided below and at the end of every 24–hour period give yourself a rating from 1 to 5 for how well you applied each of the techniques.

5 = Very Well, 4 = Well, 3 = Average, 2 = Poorly, 1 = Very Poorly.

(1) _____

(2) _____

(3) _____

Day	1st Technique	2nd Technique	3rd Technique
1	[ ]	[ ]	[ ]
2	[ ]	[ ]	[ ]
3	[ ]	[ ]	[ ]
4	[ ]	[ ]	[ ]
5	[ ]	[ ]	[ ]
6	[ ]	[ ]	[ ]
7	[ ]	[ ]	[ ]
8	[ ]	[ ]	[ ]

9	[ ]	[ ]	[ ]
10	[ ]	[ ]	[ ]
11	[ ]	[ ]	[ ]
12	[ ]	[ ]	[ ]
13	[ ]	[ ]	[ ]
14	[ ]	[ ]	[ ]
15	[ ]	[ ]	[ ]
16	[ ]	[ ]	[ ]
17	[ ]	[ ]	[ ]
18	[ ]	[ ]	[ ]
19	[ ]	[ ]	[ ]
20	[ ]	[ ]	[ ]
21	[ ]	[ ]	[ ]
22	[ ]	[ ]	[ ]
23	[ ]	[ ]	[ ]
24	[ ]	[ ]	[ ]
25	[ ]	[ ]	[ ]
26	[ ]	[ ]	[ ]
27	[ ]	[ ]	[ ]
28	[ ]	[ ]	[ ]

RULES FOR SNACKING

Write your personal Rules for Snacking in the spaces below

WHERE: _____

WHEN: _____

WHAT: _____

Give yourself a rating from 1 to 5 at the end of every 24-hour period, for how well you applied your Rules for Snacking:

5 = Very Well, 4 = Well, 3 = Average, 2 = Poorly, 1 = Very Poorly.

DAYS

1 2 3 4 5 6 7 8 9 10 11 12 13 14

DAYS
15 16 17 18 19 20 21 22 23 24 25 26 27 28

EATING TRIGGERS

1 _____

2 _____

3 _____

4 _____

5 _____

6 _____

7 _____

8 _____

9 _____

10 _____

Index